Barbarian Play:
Plautus' Roman Cor.

In this volume William S. Anderson sets Plautus, Rome's earliest surviving poet, in his rightful place among the Greek and Roman writers of what we know as New Comedy (fourth to second centuries BC).

Anderson begins by defining major innovations that Plautus made on inherited Greek New Comedy (Menander, Philemon, and Diphilus), transforming it from romantic domestic drama to a celebration of rollicking family anarchy. He shows how Plautus diminished the traditional importance of love and replaced it with a new major theme: 'heroic badness,' especially embodied in the rogue slave (ancestor of the impudent servant, valet, or maid). Anderson then examines the unique verbal texture of Plautus' drama and demonstrates his revolt against realism, his drive to have his characters defy everyday circumstances and pit their intrepid linguistic wit against social order, their Roman extravagant impudence against Greek self-control.

Finally, Anderson explores the special form of metatheatre that we admire in Plautus, by which he undermines the assumptions of his Greek 'models' and replaces them with a new, confident Roman comedy.

WILLIAM S. ANDERSON is Professor of Classics and Comparative Literature at the University of California, Berkeley. Among his other books are *Essays on Roman Satire* and *Ovidius Metamorphoses*.

THE ROBSON CLASSICAL LECTURES

William S. Anderson, *Barbarian Play: Plautus' Roman Comedy*

Alexander Dalzell, *The Criticism of Didactic Poetry* (forthcoming)

Niall Rudd, *The Classical Tradition in Operation* (forthcoming)

WILLIAM S. ANDERSON

Barbarian Play: Plautus' Roman Comedy

UNIVERSITY OF TORONTO PRESS

Toronto Buffalo London

© University of Toronto Press Incorporated 1993
Toronto Buffalo London
Printed in Canada
Paperback edition 1996
0-8020-7941-5

Printed on acid-free paper

Canadian Cataloguing in Publication Data

Anderson, William S. (William Scovil), 1927–
Barbarian play: Plautus' Roman comedy

(The Robson classical lectures; 1)
Includes bibliographical references and index.

ISBN 0-8020-2815-2 (bound)
ISBN 0-8020-7941-5 (pbk.)

1. Plautus, Titus Maccius – Criticism and interpretation
I. Title II. Series.

PA6585.A53 1993   872'.01   C93-093219-6

This book has been published with
the help of a grant from the
Canadian Federation for the Humanities,
using funds provided by the
Social Sciences and Humanities Research
Council of Canada.

Contents

Foreword

With this volume we inaugurate the Robson Classical Lectures. Donald Oakley Robson (1905–76) graduated in Honours Classics from Victoria College in the University of Toronto in 1928, and earned his MA (1929) and his PhD (1932) from the University of Toronto. After teaching at the University of Western Ontario for seventeen years, he returned to his *alma mater*, and taught Latin there from 1947 until his retirement in 1975. His wife, Rhena Victoria Kendrick (1901–82), also graduated in Honours Classics from Victoria College, in 1923, with the Governor General's Gold Medal. They were generous benefactors of their college. In Professor Robson's will he made provision that, from time to time, a series of public lectures should be delivered on a classical theme by a distinguished scholar, and then, after appropriate revision, published.

This series will, we believe, have a broad appeal among those who are interested in ancient Greece and Rome, and in the culture of classical antiquity. When the Committee was beginning to arrange the practical details, we wanted to find a scholar of reputation to deliver several lectures that would be intelligible to a non-specialist audience, and yet would at the same time provide the basis for a sound, scholarly, innovative book. A difficult assignment, to be sure! But the Committee at once unanimously agreed upon Professor William S. Anderson (of the University of California at Berkeley), and invited him to give the first Robson Classical Lectures. He graciously consented, and in October 1987 he came to Toronto, and presented three public lectures on 'The Comedies of Plautus.' The Committee agreed with him that it would be desirable to add annotation and several further chapters before publication.

We now present the first volume of the Robson Classical Lectures, a distinguished contribution to what we are confident will become a distinguished series.

The Committee expresses its gratitude to the successive presidents of Victoria University, Goldwin S. French and Eva Kushner, for their encouragement and support.

Wallace McLeod
for the Committee, 1993

MEMBERS OF THE COMMITTEE

J.M. Bigwood, 1984–93; *Chairman* 1985–6

A.M. Keith, 1989–93

G.L. Keyes, 1984–5

W.E. McLeod, 1984–93; *Chairman* 1989–93

D.P. de Montmollin, 1984–5

K.R. Thompson, 1984–93

J.S. Traill, 1984–93; *Chairman* 1984–5, 1986–9

J.N. Grant, *ex officio*, 1984–6

C.P. Jones, *ex officio*, 1986–9

E.I. Robbins, *ex officio*, 1989–93

Preface

Comedy has always been a problem for critical discussion, not only because of the wide diversity of its types and the many preconceived definitions into which critics attempt to force individual specimens, but also because the very process of critical discussion tends, all too frequently, to obscure the pleasure the dramatic performance once produced, which it is a key purpose of later readers to recover. Among classical comic playwrights, Plautus arouses the least appreciation, because his art responds most uneasily to the philological techniques which, as tools of dramatic criticism, achieve such excellent results with Menander, Terence, and even Aristophanes. Recent books, notably those of Segal, Wright, Slater, and Konstan, have done much to place Plautus squarely at the heart of the Roman tradition of comedy, to focus proper attention on the anarchic kind of humour and social commentary that joyously fills his lines, and to view his self-conscious, audience-directed drama in terms of the metatheatrical techniques so dear to modern critics. It is the purpose of this book to bring some of these separate emphases together and to insist, for Latinists and general readers alike, on the special genius of Plautus, uniquely successful in his day, uniquely available today as evidence of a particularly high point of early Roman achievement in rivalry with prior Greek mastery. If, as he ironically put it, from the Greek perspective he turned those Greek originals into something barbaric (*Plautus vortit barbare*), from the Roman and Plautine perspective his 'barbarian play' was infinitely more amusing and apt for its times and culture.

I owe the beginnings of this work to Victoria College at the University of Toronto, which invited me in October 1987 to be their first Robson Lecturer. Over a most enjoyable week, during which my wife and I were treated with memorable hospitality and friendliness, I gave three lectures, which form the substance of chapters 1, 4, and 6 of this volume. Revised and supplemented with three more chapters that focus on other aspects of Plautus' art, they will, I hope, convey my enjoyment of his Roman comedy and help to bring to others similar pleasure.

I take this opportunity to pay respects to the memory of Professor D.O. Robson (1905–76), through whose bequest the lectureship was established; to thank the committee for the lecture series, John Traill and Wallace McLeod in particular, and other members of Victoria College, who all made my visit so delightful; and to recall with affection Professor George E. Duckworth, whom I first met in Rome in June 1955, shortly after he had published his monumental book, *The Nature of Roman Comedy*. With warm respect towards those I have named and the many students at the University of California at Berkeley who have read the plays of Plautus with me, I dedicate this book to my wife, Deirdre, who is the continuous inspiration of my own personal *comoedia*.

Berkeley, California   August 1989, May 1992

BARBARIAN PLAY:

PLAUTUS' ROMAN COMEDY

CHAPTER ONE

Plautus and the Deconstruction of Menander

In 1952 Professor George Duckworth of Princeton published his book *The Nature of Roman Comedy.*[1] It was a happy moment for such a study, and Duckworth's assimilation and assessment of scholarly work of the first half of the twentieth century remains a basic tool of the classicist and the informed reader of Latin comedy. The situation in 1952 was this: the Latin texts of Plautus and Terence had remained virtually unchanged, as no new manuscript evidence had been discovered since the nineteenth century; but new methods of research on dramatic techniques, comic language, and the nature of comedy had spurred detailed study of Plautus and Terence;[2] and, in 1905, for the first time since antiquity, with the recovery of the Cairo papyrus, scholars had acquired substantial amounts of the work of the Greek dramatist Menander and were thus able to begin comparison of Greek and Roman New Comedy.[3] As a result of these new Greek comparative materials and the new literary methodology for studying Plautus and Terence, classical philology had accomplished a great deal by 1952, as Duckworth's balanced critical survey amply demonstrates.

The sudden recovery of significant amounts of Menander's work was a most welcome event in 1905, and it inspired many scholars, young and old. However, the recovered Menander proved far from satisfactory or adequate to the extensive purposes of comparison. Most particularly, none of the four Greek plays that were partially rescued was directly related to the twenty-one Plautine or six Terentian plays that manuscripts have preserved.

Then, none of the four plays was even close to complete. Perhaps three-quarters of one comedy, less than half of two, and
barely fifty lines of a fourth constituted the new Menander.[4] In the
case of the three better-preserved plays, accident had robbed
scholars of both the beginnings and the endings, and much was
uncertain about the plot and structure. Thus, although scholar-
ship produced magnificent results with this Menandrian find, it
had to stop in caution and frustration at many points. This caution is reflected in Duckworth's survey: he shows great reserve
about claiming very much for Menander as a predecessor of
Terence, let alone Plautus.[5] Even so, some of the statements he
does risk about what Menander could and could not do, while
likely enough in 1952, have been demonstrated to be wrong by
subsequent discoveries.

Before the decade of the 1950s ended, the long-extant vacuum
in Menandrian material suddenly began to be filled. A Swiss
collector of papyrus acquired a virtually complete early comedy,
usually called by translators *The Grouch*, and it was first published in swift order in 1959. There followed twenty years of
major and minor finds, which have vastly increased the amount
of Menander available to contemporary students. We now possess,
for practical purposes, two complete comedies of quite different
plots and tones; we have acquired the first half of *The Shield*,
which allows us to enjoy the first examples of a Menandrian
villain and a clever slave; and, in a short fragment of 110 lines
from *The Double-Deceiver*, Professor Handley, then of London
University, recognized in 1968 the source from which Plautus
adapted a section of his *Bacchis-Sisters*.[6]

This second Menander bonanza encourages us to assess with
greater confidence his role as a prototype of Plautus, who is my
subject, to attempt to define the goals and achievement of the
Roman poet against those of the Greek. I have chosen a flamboyant and polemical subtitle for this first chapter, namely, 'the
deconstruction of Menander.' The second syllable of that critical
term is supremely important to me, for I shall argue, taking
conscious liberties with the usual function of the word, not that
Menander's own plays lead to self-destruction, or that Plautus
spoiled Greek comedy by inept and sloppy acts of destruction,

but that Plautus knew what he was doing and by artful de-con-
struction shaped one kind of comedy (that admittedly served its
purposes admirably in the Athenian theatre of the fourth and
third centuries and, long after, in the Greek world, all the way to
the fifth century of our cra) into another wonderful kind of comedy that succeeded brilliantly with its Roman audiences and
continues to work today.

I propose to examine Plautus' techniques of 'deconstruction'
in connection with Menander's *Double-Deceiver* and the comedy he adapted from the Greek, *The Bacchis-Sisters*. We can start
on fairly solid ground, because, as I have indicated, since 1968
we have possessed 110 lines from the middle of the Greek comedy
that parallel Plautus' play. Those lines still remain the longest
parallel passage for any of Plautus or Terence – twenty-seven
comedies. I shall discuss only fifty-one lines of the Menander,
half of the material recovered. The remaining fifty-nine lines are
so fragmentary that many still have not been published and so
would add little. Moreover, except for the first ten lines, which
definitely parallel a scene in Plautus, we are not seriously incon-
venienced by the large gap from line 31 to line 90; for, as I shall
soon emphasize, those sixty lines contained two short scenes that
Plautus decided to eliminate from his own play. We begin with the
scenes preserved in lines 11–30 (Figure 1, pp. 6–7) of the Greek.[7]

Here is the dramatic situation devised by Menander. Young
Sostratos has been sent across the Aegean from Athens by his
father, to collect a debt. In Ephesos, he did that business all
right, but he also did a few things not planned or desired by his
father; that is, he fell in love with a prostitute who was already
contracted to serve the desires of a soldier for a year. (The girl
was probably temporarily available while the soldier was on
campaign. Even so, the fact that she encouraged Sostratos and
took his money says much about her mercenary nature and his
folly.) In due course, the soldier returned for his prostitute and
set sail for another campaign, planning to make a short stop en
route with her in Athens. Totally bewitched, Sostratos has written to his friend in Athens, Moschos, a young romantic like
himself, and asked him to locate the girl; he will arrive home
soon. Moschos has done so, but further complications have arisen

Figure 1   The Soliloquy of Sostratos in Menander

MENANDER

ΜΟΣΧΟΥ ΠΑΤΕΡ   ΛΥΔΟΣ   ΣΩΣΤΡΑΤΟΣ

11   Μ.Π.   σ]ὺ δ' ἐκεῖνον ἐκκάλει
            ]ν, νουθέτει δ' ἐναν[τίον
      αὑτόν τε σῶσον, οἰκίαν θ' ὅλην φίλων.
      Λυδέ, προάγωμεν. ΛΥ. εἰ δὲ κἀμὲ καταλίποις ...
15   Μ.Π. προάγωμεν· ἱκανὸς οὗτος αὐτῶι. ΛΥ. Σώστρατε,
      χρῆσαι πικρῶς, ἔλαυν' ἐκεῖνον τὸν ἀκρα[τῆ.
      ἅπαντας αἰσχύνει γὰρ ἡμᾶς τοὺς φίλους. –
      ΣΩ. ἤδη 'στιν οὗτος φροῦδος; ἐνπλη[
      τούτου καθέξει, Σώστρατον προήρπασας,
20   ἀρνήσεται μέν, οὐκ ἄδηλόν ἐστί μοι
      (ἰταμὴ γάρ) εἰς μέσον τε πάντες οἱ θεοὶ
      ἥξουσι. μὴ τοίνυν [.]ον[   ] νὴ Δία
      κακὴ κακῶς τοίνυν ... ἐ[π]άν[αγε, Σ]ώστρατε·
      ἴσως σε πείσει· δοῦλο[   ]ρα[
25   ἐγὼ μάλισθ', ἡ δ' ὡ[ς κενὸν συ]μπεισάτω
      ἔχοντα μηδ[έν· πᾶν ἀποδώσω τ]ῶι πατρὶ
      τὸ χ]ρυσίον· πιθαν[ευομέν]η γὰρ παύσεται
      ὅταν] ποτ αἴσθητα[ι, τὸ τῆς πα]ροιμίας,
      νεκρῶι] λέγουσα [μῦθον, ἀλλ'] ἤδη [με] δεῖ
30   ἐλθεῖν ἐπ' ἐ]κεῖνον, [ἀλλ' ὁρῶ γὰ]ρ τ[ουτο]νί

Figure 2   Soliloquy of Mnesilochus [= Sostratos] in Plautus

      PH. Mnesiloche, hoc tecum oro ut illius animum atque
                                      ingenium regas;
495   serua tibi sodalem ét mihi filium.   MN. factum uolo.
      LY. melius multo, me quoque una si cum illoc reliqueris.
      PH. adfatim est.   LY. Mnesiloche, cura, i, concastiga hominem
                                      probe,
      qui dedecorat te, me, amicum atque alios flagitiis suis.
      in te ego hoc onus omne impono.   PH. Lyde, sequere hac me.
                                      LY. sequor. –

DIS EXAPATON

FATHER OF MOSCHOS LYDOS SOSTRATOS

11 F.M.   ] You call him out
               ] and rebuke him face to face,
  And save him and his whole household of friends.
  Lydus, let's go. LY. But if you left me also ...
15 F.M. Let's go. He's quite enough. LY. Well, Sostratos.
  Pursue the libertine and treat him harshly.
  For he disgraces all of us his friends –
  SO. Is he gone now? [
  She'll hold him. You grabbed Sostratos before.
20 She will deny it, that's quite plain to me
  (She's shameless) and all the gods will be brought in
  To witness. So don't [   ] by Zeus.
  The devil take her! Careful, Sostratos.
  She'll perhaps persuade you. [I'm her] slave [
  But let her persuade me when I'm [empty-handed],
25 And penniless. [I'll pay back all] the gold
  To father. Then she'll stop beguiling me,
  When she perceives that, as the proverb has it,
  She's telling [tales to a corpse]. But I must go
30 And find him now. [Why, here he comes.]

PH. Try, Mnesilochus, I beg you, to reform his mind and
                                heart;
495 Save yourself a friend and me a son. MN. I'll do it willingly.
  LY. Better far though if you left *me* also here along with *him*.
  PH. He will do. LY. Take charge, Mnesilochus, castigate the
                              fellow well:
  By his scandals he's disgracing you, me, and his other friends. –
  I rely entirely on you. PH. Lydus, follow me. LY. I will.

Figure 2 (*continued*)

MNESILOCHVS

500 MN.   Inimiciorem nunc utrum credam magis
    sodalemne esse an Bacchidem incertum admodumst.
    illum exoptauit potius ? habeat.   optumest.
    ne illa illud hercle cum malo fecit suo;
    nam mihi diuini numquam quisquam creduat,
505 ni ego illam exemplis plurumis planeque – amo.
    ego faxo hau dicet nactam quem derideat.
    nam iam domum ibo atque – aliquid surrupiam patri.
507ᵃ id istí dabo.   ego istanc multis ulciscar modis.
    adeo égo illam cogam usque ut mendicet – meu' pater.
    sed satine ego animum mente sincera gero,
510 qui ad hunc modum haec hic quae futura fabulor?
    amo hercle opino, ut pote quod pro certo sciam.
    uerum quam illa umquam de mea pecunia
    ramenta fiat plumea propensior,
    mendicum malim mendicando uincere.
515 numquam edepol uiua me inridebit.   nam mihi
    decretumst renumerare iam omne aurum patri.
    igitur mi inani atque inopi subblandibitur
    tum quom mihi nihilo pluris [blandiri] referet,
    quam si ad sepulcrum mortuo narret logos.
519ᵃ sed autem quam illa umquam meis opulentiis
519ᵇ ramenta fiat grauior aut propensior,
519ᶜ mori me malim l excruciatum l inopia.
510 profecto stabilest me patri aurum reddere.
    eadem exorabo Chrysalo caussa mea
    pater ne noceat neu quid ei suscenseat
    mea caussa de auro quod eum ludificatus est;
    nam illi aequomst me consulere, qui caussa mea
525 mendacium ei dixit.   uos me sequimini. –

MNESILOCHVS

500 I'm quíte uncértain whích of the twó to thínk
My greater enemy, Bacchis or my friend.
She fancied him more? Let her have him. Fine!
By god, someone will pay for this ... yes. I will.
Let no-one ever trust my plighted troth.
505 If I don't absolutely utterly ... love her.
She shall not say she's got a man to laugh at:
507 I'll go straight home and ... steal something from father
To give her. I'll get revenge in many ways.
508 I'll bring her right to beggary ... my father's.
But am I in possession of my senses
510 To prattle on on what is going to happen?
By god, I love her, as sure as I can be.
But rather than increase her weight of wealth
By a feather's fluff from any money of mine,
I'd choose to outdo beggars in beggary.
515 By heaven she'll never live to laugh at me.
I'll pay back all the gold to father: that's decided.
When I'm poor and empty-handed, she can wheedle me.
For then her wheedling will be no more use
519 Than telling tales to a dead man in his grave.
[But rather than see her more weighted down
Or heavier by a scrap from wealth of mine.
I'd rather die in anguished poverty.]
520 My mind's made up: I'll hand the gold to father.
I'll also beg him not to punish Chrysalus
For my sake, nor to be enraged at all
At being duped about the gold for my sake;
It's right I should protect the man who lied
525 To him for my sake. You there, follow me. –

that have trapped him, too, in the situation and are about to create the crisis of our passage. It turns out that the girl from Ephesos has a sister, also a prostitute, who operates in Athens, closely resembles her, and uses the same name (at least, according to Plautus – we do not actually know what names Menander gave the two sisters). Moschos, then, tracks down Sostratos' beloved at her sister's home and quickly falls in love with the extremely seductive and ingratiating Athenian sister.

What Sostratos hopes to do is buy up the remainder of his girl's contract with the soldier and reserve her entirely for himself. Naturally, that costs money, and there is no other source of funds for this helpless lover except the money he has supposedly collected in Ephesos and is bringing back to his father. His audacious slave, Syros, concocts a deceptive tale, which serves to explain why the money has been left on deposit in Ephesos and not brought home, and for the time being Sostratos has plenty of ill-gotten funds. Shortly before our lines begin, he has returned to Athens with his secret store of cash; he has learned with pleasure that Moschos has located the girl; but as he heads for his house, he overhears an animated conversation between Moschos' father and angry tutor. The tutor is furious that he has lost control over young Moschos and cannot employ his usual severity to get anywhere against the allure of sex, and he is informing Moschos' father of the disgrace to the family. Sostratos, thinking that Moschos is merely covering for him and his Ephesian girlfriend, emerges to intercede on behalf of his chum, but the excited tutor erupts, recounting in such lurid details the lovemaking between the girl and his friend that Sostratos becomes enraged in his turn, for ironically different reasons. He cares nothing about whether or not Moschos has betrayed the tutor's teaching and the family honour, but he seethes at the thought that Moschos and the girl together have betrayed him and his love. Thinking that Sostratos' anger springs from virtuous disapproval, as theirs does, the father and tutor urge him to go into the prostitute's house and bring Moschos to his senses, with sharp but friendly words. Lines 11–17, and presumably 1–10, contain the end of that animated scene involving these three characters. Then, father and tutor go home, and Sostratos remains, delivering the monologue preserved in lines 18–30.[8]

In Menander, this is a moment of high sentimentality. Although the audience knows that Sostratos is mistaken, the mistake is entirely understandable and the bitter disappointment of this inexperienced lover easily grasped. Wasting not a word or thought on Moschos, he focuses exclusively on the rapacious whore (as he now imagines her) who has dumped him for another lover with ready cash. All Sostratos' golden erotic expectations have vanished, and the gold he has stolen from his father for the girl is at risk. She is so persuasive, he feels, that, even if he goes to see her, angry and convinced of her faithlessness, she might wheedle it from him (line 24). Therefore, he makes the decision to return it to his father before he talks with her, so that he can have the pleasure of hearing her wheedle in vain.

So Menander has made the monologue quickly and brilliantly represent the bitter disappointment of Sostratos and his drastic decision to undo the deception of his slave by restoring the money to his father. He categorizes the girl as a typical whore, shameless, bad, mercenary (lines 20 ff). His chaotic emotions make him apostrophize her, address himself, imagine a meeting with her, and then finally leap to his decision. It all follows naturally, spoken as one would be likely to speak under such pressure, and Menander guarantees that his audience accepts the situation and the speaker with full sympathy. This is engrossing melodrama.

Now consider these scenes as adapted for Latin (Figure 2, pp. 6–9). The linguistic texture of the Plautine passage is quite uneven, by contrast, and it creates a distinct unreality in what is said by Mnesilochus, whose very name is an almost absurd substitute by Plautus for the conventional name Sostratos. The result of this unevenness, in turn, is incredulity and refusal of sympathy by the audience. Neither the situation nor the character seems believable to us, and Plautus invites us, rather, to laugh at the very complexity Menander had constructed to produce a high degree of appealing emotionality.

The most striking device used to produce this unevenness by the poet is what is known as the unexpected or surprise ending, indicated in the translation by the ellipses at lines 503, 505, 507, and 508. In each case, Mnesilochus starts to say what the context realistically demands (what the Greek original would have given), and suddenly he is made to break away and blurt out the comic reverse of what we expect. Thus, in line 503 he seems to threaten the girl with condign punishment, but ends by predicting that he himself will be the victim. Similarly, in line 505 we anticipate that he will use a powerful verb, conveying his determined hostility, and instead he suddenly collapses with a silly confession of his helpless love, all in the single word *amo*. Having once again declared his determination to act and not allow the girl to laugh at him (line 506), Mnesilochus confidently announces that he is going home and – but he stops, unable to articulate his plan (which emerges finally only at line 516), and instead he transfers his hostility to his poor father, as though more could be stolen from him. By line 508, he manages to state his verb, but suddenly he alters his viewpoint again and therefore changes the subject of the verb: the girl will not be beggared; his father will be.

Now, obviously a realistic and sentimentally convincing Mnesilochus would have no capacity for wit at this point. By feeding him these lines, Plautus makes him a vehicle of his and our wit, an unconscious verbalizer of his own romantic folly. Whereas Menander had sympathetically rendered the process by which Sostratos reached his resolve, Plautus expects us to ridicule – he even gives us the cue with *derideat* at line 506 – this lover who cannot make up his mind, who cannot decide whom to hate and whom to love and how to express his bitter anger. I personally believe that this is very good comic language and, acted in the right way, good for repeated laughs. But the main point I am driving at is that Plautus has constructed something quite different from that of Menander. He does not want a realistic and sympathetic speech or speaker here, and he wants us to distance ourselves from the Greek tension between passionate feelings of abused love and guilty responsibility towards one's father. Mnesilochus becomes a caricature of indecisive love, a victim of Plautus' humour. It seems likely that Plautus' original Latin text became somewhat padded in later performances, but even the original was much longer and more wordy than the tight thirteen lines of Sostratos' monologue. Plautus happily adds words to the closely structured diction of Menander in order to achieve his deconstruction and capture laughter.

In a second episode (lines 89–112, Figure 3, pp. 14–17), Menander has the two friends at last meet for the first time since the traveller left Athens. They, of course, encounter each other, but not with the equal affection that friends normally feel at such a reunion; as Moschos notes in lines 104–5, Sostratos seems glum, scowling, and even suspiciously tearful, a most unexpected contrast to Moschos' own simple pleasure in the reunion. Once again, Menander develops the scene simply, consistently, and realistically, carrying us with him in the sympathetic portrayal of friends' brief misunderstanding. As soon as his father, departing for the agora, leaves him alone (line 91), Sostratos recapitulates his bitter unhappiness, for which he holds the girl chiefly responsible, but now includes his pal Moschos in the blame (lines 99 ff). This then prepares us for his glum, unfriendly greeting of Moschos at line 104. In only six lines, Menander makes the problem clear: Sostratos erroneously believes that Moschos has done him dirt, and, as Moschos protests his innocence, the Greek text breaks off. But, to judge from Plautus, the truth about the existence of the sister and the loyalty of Moschos was quickly established, for Menander was interested in the friends' disagreement not for itself, but as a plot complication that aborted one deception and thus necessitated the double deception of his title.

The Plautine adaptation begins at line 530 (Figure 4, pp. 16–19). Once again, Plautus has deconstructed Menander by comically verbalizing the dramatic situation and thus distancing us and our feelings from the characters. However, he does not resort to the same technique: Plautus has, in fact, a vast repertoire of comic de-constructive devices. Menander has handed him a situation of misunderstanding, and that is too tempting to the Roman sense of irreverence and laughing incredulity. So Plautus sets out to exaggerate and prolong the misunderstanding. We can see this intention from the start, in the way the two young men make contact. Plautus inserts a line that varies the usual stage direction of his plays – there's so-and-so – and has Mnesilochus deny (without having heard Pistoclerus' line) that Pistoclerus is his buddy: no, he's his enemy (line 534). After more stage directions

Figure 3   End of Act II, Beginning of Act III, in Menander

ΣΩΣΤΡΑΤΟΥ ΠΑΤΗΡ   ΣΩΣΤΡΑΤΟΣ

52   Σ.Π   ]σα· τ[ὸ χρυ]σίον [δό]θ᾽ ὑμεῖς, παῖ, ταχύ.
     ΣΩ. λήψει π]αρ᾽ [ἡ]μῶν· μὴ πρόσεχε κενῶι λόγωι.
     οὐδεὶς] παρώρμησ᾽ οὐδ᾽ ἐπεβούλευσ᾽ οὐδὲ εἷς.
55   Σ.Π. οὐ πρὸς Θ]εότιμον κατετέθη τὸ χρυσίον;
     ΣΩ. τί πρὸς Θεότιμον; αὐτὸς ἐφύλαττεν λαβὼν
     τ]ό τε πρὸς βίον διφορεῖ, πάτερ. Σ.Π. χρηστὸς σφόδρα·
     ἐφ[ρόντι]σέ τι. τί οὖν ὁ Σύρος ἐβούλετο;
     ΣΩ. ἐ[ατέο]ν. μετ᾽ ἐμοῦ δ᾽ ἀκολούθει καὶ λαβέ
60   τὸ χρυσίον. Σ.Π. παίζεις; ΣΩ. ἀκολούθει καὶ λαβέ.
     Σ.Π. οὐκοῦν ἀκολουθῶ· δὸς μόνον, καλῶς τέ μοι
     ὡς [δεῖ] κέχρησαι· πρὶν λαβεῖν μάχομαι τί σοι;
     ἐμοὶ δὲ πάντων τοῦτο προὐργιαίτερον. –

Χ Ο Ρ Ο Υ
ΣΩΣΤΡΑΤΟΣ   ΣΩΣΤΡΑΤΟΥ ΠΑΤΗΡ   ΜΟΣΧΟΣ

89   ΣΩ.   ].μοι. Σ.Π. ταῦτ᾽ ἄπειμι πρὸς ἀγορὰν
90   πρ]άττ[ων. ὃ] τι πράττηις ἄλλο δέδοται τοῦτό σοι. –
     ΣΩ. κα]ὶ μ[ὴν δο]κῶ μοι τὴν καλήν τε κἀγαθὴν
     ἰδεῖν ἐρωμένην ἂν ἡδ[έ]ως κενὸς
     πιθανευομένην καὶ προσδοκῶσαν (᾽αὐτίκα᾽
     φησὶν δ᾽ ἐν αὑτῆι) πᾶν ὃ κομίζω χρυσίον.
95   ᾽πάνυ γὰρ κομίζει τοῦτο καί, νὴ τοὺς θεούς.
     ἐλευθερίως (τίς μᾶλλον;) ἀξίως τ᾽ ἐμοῦ.᾽
     αὑτη δ᾽ ἱκανῶς, καλῶς ποοῦσά γ᾽, εὑρέθη
     οἵαν ποτ᾽ ὦιμην οὖσα, τὸν δ᾽ ἀβέλτερον
     Μόσχον ἐ[λ]ε[ῶ]: καὶ τὰ μὲν ἔγωγ᾽ ὀργίζομαι,
100 τὰ δ᾽ οὐκ ἐκεῖνον τοῦ γεγονότος αἴτιον
     ἀδικήματος νενόμικα, τὴν δ᾽ ἰταμωτάτην
     πασῶν ἐκείνην. ΜΟ. εἶτ᾽ ἀκούσας ἐνθάδε
     εἶναί με, ποῦ γῆς ἐστι; χαῖρε, Σώστρατε.
     ΣΩ. καὶ σύ. ΜΟ. τί κατηφὴς καὶ σκυθρωπός, εἰπέ μοι;
105 καὶ βλέμμα τοῦθ᾽ ὑπόδακρυ· μὴ νεώτερον
     κακὸν κατείληφάς τι τῶν [γ᾽] ἐνταῦθα; ΣΩ. ναί.
     ΜΟ. εἶτ᾽ οὐ λέγεις; ΣΩ. ἔνδον γὰρ ἀμέλει, Μόσχε. ΜΟ. πῶς;

FATHER OF SOSTRATOS   SOSTRATOS

52 F.S.   ] hand over the gold, son, quickly.
    SO. You'll get it] from us. Ignore that idle tale.
    For no-one anchored near or plotted against us.
55 F.S. Was the gold not left then with Theotimos?
    SO. With Theotimos? No, but *he* took charge of it.
    He's good with money, father. F.S. Excellent.
    That was wise of him. So what was Syrus up to?
    SO. Forget it. Come along with me and get
60 The gold. F.S. You're joking? SO. Come along and get it.
    F.S. I'm coming. Just pay up and you'll have done
    Your duty well. Why quarrel before I get it?
    That is the most important thing for me. –

CHORUS

SOSTRATOS FATHER OF SOSTRATOS MOSCHOS

89 SO.   ] to me. F.S. Well, I'll away to [my] business
90 At the market. You have something else to do. –
    SO. Indeed, I think I'd like to see my fine
    And noble mistress now I'm empty-handed,
    Beguiling and expecting ('any moment'
    She says to herself) the sum of gold I'm bringing.
95 'I'm sure he's bringing it, by heaven. There's none
    More generous, and it's just as I deserve.'
    She's now been clearly shown (and serve her right)
    To be what I once thought her. But I [pity]
    The poor fool Moschos. Yes, in a way I'm angry,
100 But I don't consider *him* to be the cause
    Of the mischief that's been done, but *her*, the most
    Shameless of hussies. MO. If he's heard I'm here,
    Where on earth is he? Oh, greetings, Sostratos.
    SO. Greetings. MO. But, tell me, why these scowls and frowns?
105 And why this tearful look? I trust you haven't
    Picked up some trouble locally. SO. I have.
    MO. Well, tell me. SO. It's in there, of course. MO. How so?

Figure 3 (*continued*)

ΣΩ.]φιλοῦντα τὸν πρὸ τοῦ χρόνον
      ]α· τοῦτο πρῶτον ὧν ἐμὲ
110   ]ἠδίκηκας. ΜΟ. ἠδίκηκα δὲ
ἐγώ σε; μὴ γένοιτο τοῦτο, Σώστρατε.
ΣΩ. οὐκ ἠξίουν γοῦν οὐδ᾽ ἐγώ. ΜΟ. λέγεις δὲ τί;

Figure 4 Plautus' Treatment of the Act-break and of the Disagreement of Friends

---

PISTOCLERVS

526 PI. Rebus aliis anteuortar, Bacchis, quae mandas mihi:
Mnesilochum ut requiram atque ut eum mecum ad te ad-
                                          ducam simul.
nam illud animus meu' miratur, si a me tetigit nuntius,
quid remoretur. ibo ut uisam huc ad eum, si forte est domi.

MNESILOCHVS PISTOCLERVS

530 MN. Reddidi patri I omne aurum. nunc ego illam me uelim
conuenire, postquam inanis sum, contemptricem meam.
sed ueniam mi quam grauate pater dedit de Chrysalo!
uerum postremo impetraui ut ne quid ei suscenseat.
PI. estne hic meu' sodalis? MN. estne hic hostis quem
                                          aspicio meus?
535 PI. certe is est. MN. is est. adibo contra et contollam gradum.
PI. saluos sis, Mnesiloche.   MN. salue.   PI. saluos quom
                                          peregre aduenis,
cena detur. MN. non placet mi cena quae bilem mouet.
PI. numquae aduenienti aegritudo obiecta est?   MN. atque
                                          acerruma.
PI. unde? MN. ab homine quem mi amicum esse arbitratus
                                          sum antidhac.
540 PI. multi more isto atque exemplo uiuont, quos quom censeas
esse amicos, reperiuntur falsi falsimoniis,
lingua factiosi, inertes opera, sublesta fide.
nullus est quoi non inuideant rem secundam optingere;
sibi ne ínuideatur, ipsi ígnaui recte cauent.

SO. You are the man I [thought] my friend before,
And now I find you've deceived me.] That's the first
110 Of all our dealings where] you've wronged me. MO. What?
I've wronged you? Heaven forbid it, Sostratos!
SO. I didn't expect it either. MO. What d'you mean?

PISTOCLERUS

526 PI. Yoúr instrúctions wíll take précedence, Bácchis, óver óther
things.
I will try to find Mnesilochus and then bring him back to you.
For to my mind it's a mystery, if my message did arrive.
What's delaying him. I'll pay a call in here in case he's home.

MNESILOCHUS PISTOCLERUS

530 MN. Wéll, I've hánded óver áll the góld to fáther. Nów I'd líke
Her to meet me, my contemptress, in my empty-handed state.
How reluctant, though, my father was to pardon Chrysalus!
But I managed to persuade him not to be enraged at all.
PH. Can it be my friend there? MN. Can it be my enemy I see?
535 PI. Yes it is. MN. It is. PI. Well, I'll approach him. MN. I'll
confront him, then.
PI. Ah Mnesilochus, greetings. MN. Greetings. PI. Now you're
back from overseas
Safely, you must come to dinner. MN. Not to one which stirs
my bile.
PI. Have you picked up some complaint then on return? MN.
A painful one.
PI. What's the cause? MN. A man I thought till now to be a
friend of mine.
540 PI. What you say suggests a pattern by which many people
live:
Friends you think them, but in practice by their falsehoods
they're proved false
Busy-tongued but slow to action, fickle in their promises.
No-one can escape their envy when prosperity befalls;
They themselves, though, are so idle, no-one else need envy
them.

Figure 4 *(continued)*

545 MN. edepol ne tu illorum mores perquam meditate tenes.
   sed etiam unum hoc : ex ingenio malo malum inueniunt suo :
   nulli amici sunt, inimicos ipsi in sese omnis habent.
   atque i se quom frustrant, frustrari alios stolidi existumant.
   sicut est hic quem esse amicum ratu' sum atque ipsus sum

mihi:

550 ille, quod in se fuit, accuratum habuit quod posset mali
   faceret in me, inconciliaret copias omnis meas.
   PI. inprobum istunc esse oportet hominem.   MN. égo ita

esse arbitror.

   PI. opsecro hercle loquere, quis is est.   MN. beneuolens

uiuit tibi.

   nam ni ita esset, tecum orarem ut ei quod posses mali
555 facere faceres. PI. dic modo hominem qui sit : si non fecero
   ei male aliquo pacto, me esse dicito ignauissumum.
   MN. nequam homost, uerum hercle amicus est tibi.

PI. tanto magis

   dic quis est : nequám hominis ego parui pendo gratiam.
   MN. uideo non potesse quin tibi eius nomen eloquar.
560 Pistoclere, perdidisti me sodalem funditus.

545 MN. Well, by heaven, you've grasped their character, very
                                        comprehendingly.
    One thing more though: evil natures bring their own evil
                                        rewards.
    They've no friends themselves, since they make enemies of
                                        everyone.
    Stupidly they think they're cheating others when they cheat
                                        themselves.
    Like the man I thought my friend, as much my friend as I
                                        myself;
550 Who, by all the means at his disposal, set himself to do
    All the harm to me he could, and commandeer my property.
    PI. He must be an utter scroundrel. MN. That's what I regard
                                        him as.
    PI. Tell me, then, for god's sake, who he is. MN. A wellwisher
                                        of yours.
    If he weren't, I'd beg you do him all the mischief which you
                                        were
555 Capable of doing. PI. Tell me who he is, and if I don't
    Do him some kind of a mischief, call me the most worthless
                                        wretch.
    MN. He's a villain, and a friend of yours, by heaven. PI. So
                                        much the more,
    Tell me who. A villain's favour doesn't rank so high with me.
    MN. Well, I see there's nothing for it but to speak his name to
                                        you.
560 Pistoclerus, you have ruined me, your best friend, utterly.

in line 535, the two exchange greetings, Mnesilochus in a cold and laconic manner. According to a standard formula of Plautus, a returning traveller should be invited to dinner by his friends, and Pistoclerus does so, but the invitation is refused in a way that both expresses Mnesilochus' hostility and puzzles Pistoclerus, who has acted with honest enthusiasm. Why does the thought of dinner make Mnesilochus sick? Whereas Menander gives no stage directions in his text until Moschos describes his friend's look, Plautus writes into his comedy a variety of strong verbalizations of enmity.

These initial tactics serve only to introduce the major expansion. As Barsby interprets the somewhat fragmentary Greek of lines 108–10, Sostratos simply blurts out what bothers him, after one brief hesitation in line 107: he thought Moschos was his friend, but now, he directly accuses Moschos, you have done me wrong. What Plautus does is to draw out Mnesilochus' anger and Pistoclerus' bewilderment by transforming Menander's clearly attributed remark about the friend who betrayed (namely, Moschos/ Pistoclerus) into an ambiguous statement that seems to Pistoclerus quite naturally to be about someone else. Mnesilochus deliberately exploits the ambiguity to confuse Pistoclerus and cleverly lead him by the nose for a while. This is good for twenty lines (539–59) of smart deception, which Mnesilochus and the audience (and obviously Plautus) enjoy for itself. That Mnesilochus falls out of character in the process is no objection for Plautus: on the contrary, it is his goal to deconstruct the sentimental scene and the audience's sympathetic identification with the characters and situation. His Mnesilochus does not really feel any anguish, and he is not allowed to play a consistent role. As in his preceding speech he blew his chance quite impudently to be a convincing lover, here he fools away what he so exaggeratedly announces as 'hostility' at his first sight of Pistoclerus.

One additional point about the texture, the new construction of Plautus' verses in lines 530 ff: whereas Menander has used a uniform iambic trimeter throughout lines 1–110 to convey a common level of everyday communication, Plautus uses trochaic septenarius for the scene before Mnesilochus' monologue (494–9) and for the dialogue scene that we have been discussing (530 ff). You can spot the rhythmic difference in the translation; in Roman drama, that difference was emphasized, because the actor spoke the iambic lines much as we do blank verse, whereas the trochaic septenarius, accompanied by the flute, sounded more like operatic recitative. Now, if the dialogue between Mnesilochus and Pistoclerus were played straight, I dare say that such a metre would be conveying some of the special intensity of Menander's short scene. As it is, however, the 'operatic' overtones of the metre instead serve to emphasize the irreverence of text and characters, and so ultimately of Plautus. Pistoclerus is having a wonderful time waxing unconvincingly sententious, and Mnesilochus is enjoying himself even more, solemnly teasing additional nonsense from his supposed enemy. We now know that, for very special scenes, Menander did switch from iambics to trochaics, namely, for especially powerful episodes at the emotional climax of a play.[9] However, Menander had reached no such climax here, and stays in iambic. We might suggest that Plautus' decision to use the verbose and musically animated trochees represents a deliberate anticlimax. His comedies are full of such anticlimax.

So far, we have concentrated on the verbal and metrical texture of three sections (two of them incomplete episodes) in the Greek fragment and Plautus' deconstructive adaptation. We have seen how the Roman comedy keeps interrupting and upsetting the sentimental seriousness of the original Greek, how the characters seem to know that they are actors and exaggerate their postures, overstate the tensions of the scene, and riot in words. The agony of love, the bitter distrust of girlfriend and long-time chum, which form the thematic framework of Menander's lines, become in Plautus the motivation for insouciant wit. Now, it is time to look at the larger structure and Plautus' continuous procedures of deconstruction.

Consider the two scenes of Menander (lines 30–90) that Plautus cut. At line 30 of the Greek, Sostratos declares his intention to go find his father. The elder is not at home, but at the agora, looking for his son. As Sostratos starts off stage, a standard device of dramatic economy brings the father on, so the wished-for meeting quickly takes place before the audience. When the text continues, the son is reassuring his father that the slave's story was a fiction and that the money has come home and is available. The two hurry back into their home for the money. Here, Menander marked an act-break and indicated a choral interlude, which helped to suggest the passage of time. When the chorus departed, the same two characters emerged from the house. Almost thirty lines of Greek, very fragmentary in their present condition, have never been published, but scholars assume reasonably that the father voiced his mixed emotions about recovering his funds and about the rascally slave Syros, who had deceived him. Sostratos did not tell the whole truth about why he wanted the money, but he did intercede on behalf of his slave and get his parent reluctantly to agree not to punish Syros. At line 89, the father prepares to return to the agora, to put his money into safe keeping, and at line 90 he leaves Sostratos to his private affairs. Plautus has eliminated both these scenes between father and son, but briefly summarized what Mnesilochus intends at line 520 and what he has accomplished at lines 530–3.

Since up to now we have focused exclusively on Plautus' deconstructive techniques of expansion, overelaboration, and overstatement, we should ask ourselves how his deconstruction works by omission. It certainly is not enough to say that he merely cuts the scenes because he had no chorus and no act-breaks, and therefore had to find some way of maintaining continuity. Even if he inverted the order of entrance of the two young men and had Pistoclerus appear at line 526, the four lines that Pistoclerus speaks hardly cover the real time it took Mnesilochus to do his business. Plautus rarely has any interest in providing a realistic illusion of time passed. No, what Plautus wants to omit is the enactment of the relation between father and son. The published remnants of the Greek prevent us from being totally confident of how these scenes went, but what survives presents a sincere relationship, a simple give-and-take in which the Menandrian father is not overbearing and listens to the son, expresses no anger against the son but only at tricky Syros, and certainly shows no unusual avarice about the money. Both characters are sympathetic; together they symbolize the basic family unity. This pair of scenes, for Menander's play, then served an important function in the thematic and dramatic total structure.

As the first deception and the illicit erotic affair collapse for the first time, father and son meet and act out their unity of purpose with the symbolic return of the fraudulently obtained gold. We know that Sostratos has failed to explain his involvement with the prostitute next door, so the trust of the father is not fully deserved, nor is the affair of the heart fully resolved. But this incomplete tableau of family unity at this point in the play sets the pattern of plot and audience expectation for the next acts. As Menander's title implies and Plautus' adaptation demonstrates, Sostratos, having discovered his error about the girl, immediately recants on his family obligations and invokes the help of Syros a second time for an even more exciting bit of deception. That, in turn, should have led to the orderly fulfilment of audience expectation in a thematic and dramatic resolution where, when Sostratos faces the truth with his father, family unity is re-established and, I believe, this unwise affair with the prostitute is either suddenly terminated or given a brief but well-defined and fully accepted time limit.[10]

We do not have the end of Menander's comedy, and I am about to claim that Plautus radically altered that original ending to complete his comic deconstruction. But what evidence can I claim for my theory about Menander? I appeal to analogy, to extant plays of the Greek poet that emphasize the theme of family unity and responsible subordination of centrifugal love-passion to the well-being of the entire family, as it is regularly embodied in the father. Secondarily, I refer to the four Menandrian plays of Terence, where paternal seriousness, often after suffering some humbling ridicule for its overconfidence, is still allowed to reassert itself against irresponsible youthful libido. I believe, then, that Menander's play ended with a scene between father and son that decisively and sympathetically filled out the incomplete features of the two short scenes the Greek fragment preserves at the break between Acts II and III.

If we recall two of those surprise endings in Mnesilochus' monologue (at lines 501 and 508), we can see why Plautus eliminated an intimate and sympathetic dialogue between Mnesilochus and his father. It is counter-productive to Plautus' comic viewpoint for fathers to be chummy with their sons and for sons to exhibit a confident and affectionate feeling for their fathers. The comic war that we have seen involving lovers and friends also pits father and son against each other – to the 'death,' as some sons declare.[11] Here, Mnesilochus verbalizes his scale of values by balking at punishing his girlfriend (though he believes she deserves it) and substituting his father as victim, robbed and reduced to beggardom. And that is the role that Plautus designates for the father, Nicobulus, throughout his comedy: not a figure of respectable authority who eventually recalls his wayward son, but a dupe, the victim of trickery and the roguery of one character after another, including his son. So Plautus does not stage this encounter between father and son, because he has changed Menander's themes and characters and deconstructed the goal of the action from one of family reconciliation to one of irresponsible anarchy in the pursuit of pleasure. By omitting this encounter, Plautus also eliminates the audience's expectations for a more complete and honest encounter between Mnesilochus and Nicobulus. He knew that he was going to end his comedy without allowing father and son to meet on stage; in fact, he was going to abort such an encounter by disgracing the father at the very moment Menander was portraying the paternal authority in benevolent action to re-establish order.

Plautus spends much time on the rollicking fun of the slave's second deception; some even think that he expanded it into a third deception. At any rate, by the point where Menander closed his fourth act with a chorus, which would be about line 800 in the average Greek play, Plautus' Latin version amounts to more than 1,200 lines. One of the most delightful expansions is a lyric aria for the tricky slave as he gloats over what he has achieved and anticipates further success (lines 925–78). Not only is the spectacular lyric form unknown in any Menandrian comedy, but the self-important attitude of the slave and the conceit with which he operates – that he is the embodiment of various Greek epic heroes who captured and sacked Troy at the expense of old King Priam (who is made the equivalent of Nicobulus) – all belong to Plautus' deconstruction of Menander, not to the Greek play.

Plautus has renamed Syros, Menander's roguish slave, Chrysalus, in order that the scamp may egotistically use his name to make puns, primarily on the gold (*chrysos*, in Greek) which his deceptions win, but also on the cross (*cruci-*) to which he might be condemned for punishment.[12] When he has carried out all his deceptions, he has a sum of gold to take in to the house of the Bacchis-sisters to Mnesilochus, and the father, Nicobulus, goes off to the forum with another sum of gold, for the soldier with whom the Ephesian Bacchis has contracted. (Chrysalus has lied, telling Nicobulus that the soldier is the angry husband of the Ephesian Bacchis, eager to exact legitimate punishment from Mnesilochus for adultery.). So Nicobulus unwittingly cooperates in his own defrauding. This section in Plautus, presented in iambics, is the last relatively subdued passage in the Latin comedy, the last which even remotely preserves the spirit of Menander.

The calm and confident departure of Nicobulus to settle, he believes, the mess created by his son is matched by his wild and angry return, after he learns the truth from the soldier on paying him his money. Since this was *the* climax of Menander's comedy, and the Greek father's fury over his son's part in these deceptions would have been valid psychologically and worth dramatically emphasizing, it is perhaps not unreasonable to guess that Menander shifted here from prosaic iambs to more excited trochees. If so, Plautus will have taken his cue from the Greek, but determined to exaggerate both character and tone by exploiting a lyric metre that, to our knowledge, in New Comedy, Greek or Latin, only he employs, namely, an eight-foot anapaestic line. Moreover, Plautus makes sure that, in his song (which might remind people of certain quick-patter songs of Gilbert and Sullivan), Nicobulus says nothing of the moral issues involved, but harps on the loss of money and on the wounds to his ego inflicted by that damned slave Chrysalus. The flamboyant language and repetitiousness of the song have their usual Plautine effect: the audience enjoys the verbal display and feels no inclination to sympathize with character or situation. How could we think that it is anything but a 'performance' when, Nicobulus rages so delightfully, as in the following lines (as Barsby translates them): 'Of the fatheads, the fools, the dullards, the dolts, the blabbers, the blundering blockheads, / The mushrooms there are in the world, there have been, or are going to be in the future, / I far and away surpass the whole lot in stupidity and in slowness of wit. / I'm damned, I'm disgraced! Just to think at my age I could twice be be-fooled in this scandalous way! / And the more I reflect, the more I'm enraged at the trouble my son has created. / I'm destroyed, yes indeed, I'm torn up by the roots, I'm tortured by every torment that's known; / I am plagued by every ill that exists, I'm engulfed in every manner of doom. / I've been mangled today, and it's Chrysalus' doing; I've been pillaged, alas, and it's Chrysalus' doing. / That villain has shorn me of gold as he pleased, using clever deceits against unclever me.'[13]

Nicobulus and Pistoclerus' father, Philoxenus, storm up to the house of the two prostitutes and pound on the door, determined to drag home in disgrace their sons and the impudent slave (the latter to punishment that will match some of the metaphors used by Nicobulus just now to describe his trickery). The Athenian Bacchis answers the angry knocks, and with her sister she succeeds in blunting the anger of the fathers and their drive to assert their rightful authority over the boys and Chrysalus. In fact, they seduce the old men, in a very vivacious lyric scene that combines an opening section in bacchiacs and a final anapaestic movement (lines 1120 ff). Thus, instead of a dramatic progression that would have symbolized, as I believe Menander did, the return to responsibility and family unity – when the penitent sons and guilty slave followed the fathers out of the house of prostitution back to their own homes – Plautus' anarchic humour represents the fathers, once more suckers for deception, this time erotic, following the girls in to join their sons and Chrysalus in a celebration of irresponsibility. They have abandoned their home, its values, and the authority that it and their position in the family automatically conferred on them.

This final act, then, with its un-Menandrian lyric display and its un-Menandrian theme of domestic anarchy, is the climax of Plautus' deconstruction. His is a careful comic achievement that avails itself of many new techniques. In addition to the verbal and metrical texture, the new characterization of fathers, and the symbolic reversal of movement into the wrong house, Plautus has enriched the scene by using four speakers. Menander artfully wrote his comedies within a convention that permitted only three speakers on stage at any one time. Plautus operates under more flexible conventions, but he does not alter Greek staging, except for good reasons: this is the only scene in the entire comedy where he resorts to four speakers. The added speaker is the Bacchis from Ephesos. The two sisters plot in our hearing the seduction of the old men, choosing their respective victims, and then Bacchis of Athens confidently and successfully takes on the 'heroic' task of alluring wild Nicobulus, while her sister has little trouble with the easy-going Philoxenus.

I remind you that Menander's comedy *The Double-Deceiver* called attention to the tricky slave, whose deceptions occupy the centre of both plays, Acts II to IV in the Greek and the equivalent in the Latin. But Plautus entitled his adaptation *The Bacchis-Sisters*. That new title reflects the changed qualities of his deconstruction and the new agents of the finale: the prostitutes whose trickery surpasses the deceptions of Chrysalus and guarantees the triumph of disorder and who, unlike the sons and Chrysalus, can operate with entire freedom, unhindered by the authority of the father, master of the house and family in normal homes. In their house, the Bacchis-sisters rule, and Plautus shows the fathers, like their sons before them, bowing to the seductive authority of the sisters and, as they enter their house, meekly accepting their amatory rule.

The Athenian Bacchis watches the tamed Nicobulus, who recognizes that he has been 'enslaved,' start into her house and smilingly comments in anapaests: 'Thus the men who were lying in wait for their sons have been captured themselves very nicely' (line 1206). When she then follows him off, the stage remains empty briefly, before the entire cast emerges to declare the Plautine moral, in trochaics: 'Had these old men not been worthless from the time when they were young, / Never would their hoary heads have been disgraced like this today,' (lines 1207–8). And that is indeed what has happened in this comedy, thanks to Plautus' artful deconstruction of Menandrian language, rhythms, characters, theme, and dramatic form: old men have been disgraced, conclusively by this final act, and we are now told that, in fact, they were corrupt and worthless from youth. The decisive disgrace has been inflicted, not by a recognizable force of virtue, but by the new title roles of this play, two prostitutes. Obvious forces of corruption to the conventional mind, the two courtesans emerge as superior, in wit and vitality, to the fathers, and not in the least inferior to them in morality.

Menander died prematurely, a victim of drowning, in the late 290s. Barely forty years later, Plautus was born, and he grew up, probably like Shakespeare and Molière, in a society that was just introducing alien theatrical styles, where talented young men could explore an exciting new life as actors. Certainly, Menander was not the only Greek playwright known in Plautine Rome, but he already possessed a towering stature, which only increased in the next centuries. Therefore, it is useful to consider what Plautus had in mind and what he achieved when he decided to adapt a comedy of Menander for contemporary Roman audiences of the early second century (the date of this play).

Menander wrote for an advanced and comfortable Athens, which had, under duress, gracefully given up its former political ambitions and was settling down to urbane domestic values and moral enlightenment (influenced by the numerous philosophic sects which found their home in Athens during the fourth and third centuries). His comedy, then, tends to be serious, ethical, and domestic. Using a smooth style, colloquial but neither vulgar nor raucously comic; writing primarily in the 'prosaic' iambic trimeter; working with characters who commit themselves totally to the dramatic situation, who are believable and whose comic quality consists in mild defects of youthful irresponsibility or simple ignorance; creating in his audience a feeling of sympathy and ironic indulgence for these temporary flaws and the difficulties they briefly produce; sketching out a positively ethical plot that moves from ignorance to knowledge, from self-indulgence to reform, from family disruption to unity; ending with a symbolic scene of a son gratefully returning to paternal authority and the family circle, of a wedding or marriage saved, of a foundling finding its true parents and grandparents, of a family celebration – by these means Menander worked out a comedy that remained the paradigm for later schoolteachers, moralists, and preachers, but also a model of sensitive elegance for any true artist. It was a model Terence admiringly accepted and later Roman satirists often used.

Plautus may well have admired Menander's plays as art works, but he adapted them with a very clear sense of their alien qualities in his Rome. And I dare say that he himself entertained a view of comedy, being the man he was and living in such a different cultural environment, that differed radically from the ironic tolerance of foibles in an essentially intelligible world, which was Menander's position. In subsequent chapters I explore more fully aspects of the genius of Plautus and of the Roman audience and environment that rendered Menander's characters, themes, and ethos essentially alien in Rome of the Hannibalic War and the early second century. What I have tried to show in this first chapter is that Plautus confronted Menander's art with a special comic talent and perception that enabled him to deconstruct it into a radically different kind of comic drama, one in which style, metre, and characters work together to upset a serious, ethical, and coherent representation, but instead co-operate in creating a laughable world of wild polar oppositions; where all authority is challenged, often successfully, and the qualities we are made to admire are roguish and amoral; where the forces of law and order, as in this play, are deceived, humiliated, and finally co-opted by a slave and two impudent prostitutes.

CHAPTER TWO

si amicus Diphilo aut Philemoni es: Plautus' Exploitation of Other Writers and Features of the Greek Comic Tradition

The discovery of the papyrus fragment of *The Double-Deceiver* demonstrates conclusively that, in adapting the Greek play of Menander to Latin, Plautus worked carefully from the Greek text, available to him, it has been suggested, in the scripts of actors who came to Italy, and especially to Rome, from the Greek world. Now, it is a curious fact that, in spite of this close acquaintance with Menander's plays, Plautus nowhere names the playwright or any of the comedies that he has adapted. It was long suspected that the *Bacchides* derived from the *Double-Deceiver*, because the Latin saying split between lines 816 and 817 – 'He whom the gods love / dies a young man' – is identical with a trimeter that Stobaeus assigned without context to the Greek play. But it took the substantial papyrus parallelism with the Latin of lines 494 ff to prove the suspicion.

We might have guessed that, in his prologue, Plautus' speaker would have identified Menander as the writer of the original he has adapted. Such an identification is a common, though not universal, element of Plautine prologues. However, the prologue of the *Bacchides*, if there was one (as many scholars conjecture), was lost when several leaves containing the start of the play were somehow separated from the archetype manuscript and disappeared.

The possibility that Plautus may have mentioned Menander in that lost prologue becomes considerably less likely when his other Menandrian adaptations prove also to omit all reference to the Greek original and its writer. What is the earliest extant use of Menander by Plautus, the *Cistellaria*, presented before the Carthaginian War had ended at Zama in 202 BC, worked from the *Synaristosae*, or *Women at Breakfast Together*. We have two delayed prologues, one after the other, for this play, at lines 120 and 149 ff. They provide us much information about background details, but neither names one or the other playwright or gives the title of the Greek or Latin comedy. The same proves true of the *Stichus*, which Plautus staged in 200 BC: didascalic information added to the Ambrosian manuscript reveals that Menander's *Adelphoe* stands behind the Latin, but the text itself gives no clues as to its origins, and it dispenses with a prologue. A fourth play, the *Aulularia*, because of its initial resemblance to the plot and tone of Menander's *Grouch*, seems to many to bear the Menandrian stamp.[1] The short opening prologue does not, however, refer to its Greek original. For whatever reason, then, Plautus does not name Menander in any of his extant plays, either to give him credit for his original or to score off him as a way of emphasizing his own creativity.

The reticence vanishes in the face of other Greek playwrights and other Greek originals. The prologue of the early *Asinaria* names its source as the *Onago*, or *Ass Herd*, of Demophilos, and the prologue of the early *Miles Gloriosus* – both are prior to the *Cistellaria* – provides the title, but not the author, of the Greek original.[2] The prologue (line 53) of the *Poenulus* also gives us a Greek title, *The Carthaginian*, but no playwright. Another early play, presumably also staged during the war, the *Mercator*, states in its prologue (lines 9–10) that Philemon wrote its original under the title of *Emporos*, or *Merchant*. Some years later, the prologue of the *Trinummus* (lines 18–19) identifies Philemon's *Thensauros* as the source it adapts. Finally, the prologue of the *Rudens* (line 32) names Diphilos as author of the unnamed original; and the prologue of the *Casina* (lines 31–3) reveals that Diphilos' *Kleroumenoi* is its source and translates the Greek title, as if to suggest that Plautus' authentic title was *Sortientes, Those Who Draw Lots*. It is possible that the prologue of the *Vidularia* referred to its Greek original: Studemund thought that he detected what could be restored as the title *Schedia*, or *Raft*. Thus, although Plautus makes liberal use of Menander's originals, he never cites the Greek writer or his titles; whereas in up to eight other prologues, the name of the Greek original and, often, of the Greek playwright – and, especially for our purposes in this chapter, Menander's great rivals, Philemon and Diphilos – prominently appear. Was it perhaps because they were somewhat closer in spirit to Plautus' sense of comedy and their plays more recognizable behind the Latin adaptations?

I have cited eight Plautine prologues where information about the Greek sources, four of which are comedies by Philemon and Diphilos, occurs. So far, I have ignored the reference that I cited as part of my title for this chapter. That is unique in its location, its form, and its tone. It appears in the final fifty lines of the *Mostellaria*, or *Haunted House*; mentions two Greek playwrights, the two we shall be interested in, but neither necessarily (though possibly) as a source for this comedy; and seems to patronize them by offering to supply them needed material. Let me sketch the comic context before citing the relevant lines in full. The angry father has at last realized that he has been totally tricked (*ludificatus*, line 1147) by the impudently clever slave Tranio, and he intends to seize the rogue and inflict on him punishment that will somewhat salve his pride. However, Tranio anticipates his master's move, takes refuge on an altar, and there continues to defy the old man, still impudent. A friend of the wastrel son whom Tranio has been helping tries to intercede, and the father asks him desperately, 'What shall I do now?' Before the friend can reply, Tranio jumps in with more impudence: 'If you're a friend of Diphilos or Philemon, be sure to tell them how your slave deceived you. You'll be supplying them for their comedies first-rate deception-routines' (*si amicus Diphilo aut Philemoni es, / dicito is quo pacto tuo' te servos ludificaverit: / optumas frustrationes dederis in comoediis*, lines 1149–51).

Although in all scrupulous caution I must admit that this passage may be a translation from the Greek and reflect a situation of rivalry in the Athenian theatre of the third century, I personally believe that it is rather a self-confident intrusion of Plautus and his Tranio, both alike expressing their self-conscious sense of superiority over their ostensible 'superiors.' The friend to whom the father has, in fact, been speaking tells Tranio to shut up and quickly arranges to repay the old man for his financial losses, which in Plautus' version is really the only thing he cares about. So the intrusion does not affect the plot; rather, it serves to interrupt with laughter and express Plautine triumph over plot. He has apparently enlarged the role of Tranio (as, we shall see, he often does with slave roles adapted from Greek) and created a person of extraordinary comic vigour, who acts out a wonderful series of deceptions well beyond the range or desire of Diphilos and Philemon. Speaking through the mouth of the triumphant slave, who taunts his furious and helpless master, Plautus offers to give 'lessons' to his dead predecessors.

The relationship of Plautus to Philemon and Diphilos is an important but treacherous subject. The recovery of work of Menander in 1905 already gave us a firmer control over his art than over any other poet of New Comedy. And the additional papyri which have increased our knowledge of Menander since 1952, but in no way supplemented our data on Philemon or Diphilos, have thus magnified the gap between the situation of Menander and that of all other comic poets. We still possess nothing but unsatisfying fragments for Menander's two major rivals and thus no real control over acts or plots, or even most characters. The peculiar concerns of Athenaeus in dinners and dinner conversation determine the surviving material of Diphilos;[3] the sententious nature of Stobaeus and the limited objectives of Athenaeus account for most of the surviving Philemon. I shall not, then, be able here to cite a Greek passage parallel to Plautus' Latin from either of the Greeks, or develop it into an analysis of the comic themes which give structure to the original Greek play and therefore allow us to glimpse the 'deconstructive' methodology of the ingenious Plautus. Instead, I shall attempt to discuss a special character type that Philemon developed in some of his plays and a specially animated scene of comic 'litigation' that Diphilos used, in order to suggest that Plautus worked his deconstructive magic here, too. Thus, the triumph he expresses in the *Mostellaria* over Philemon and Diphilos may be extended to cover other features than slave-trickery: namely, the helpful friend of Philemon and high-spirited comic decision scenes in Diphilos.

Philemon's Helpful Friend:
Plautus' Alterations of a Sentimental Stereotype

In an anecdote about the circumstances of Philemon's death, which occurred, according to ancient tradition, at the advanced age of ninety-eight in about 263 BC, Apuleius praises the Greek playwright for his mastery of twelve comic characters.[4] Included in the list of twelve is one no other ancient critic has identified, namely, the helpful friend (*sodalis opitulator*). By looking carefully at the surviving material of Greek and Roman New Comedy, we are able to conclude that such a character type did indeed exist and enjoy a fairly wide distribution. Brief allusions to the role dot the plays of Menander and Plautus (from various Greek originals). In the *Bacchides* (from Menander's *Double-Deceiver*), which we considered from a different viewpoint in the previous chapter, we saw that Pistoclerus (Moschos) was helping his friend Mnesilochus (Sostratos) by locating the girl-friend who had come to Athens from Ephesos. Detained in Ephesos by his father's business, Mnesilochus did not want to lose the charming courtesan. It was not a big thing to ask of his *sodalis*, and Pistoclerus readily accomplished the commission, for which Mnesilochus was enormously grateful upon his return to Athens. A momentary complication arose, resulting from the fact that there were two sisters called Bacchis, and Pistoclerus fell in love with the other. Mnesilochus drew the wrong conclusion, ruined the first deception of his slave, and fell out briefly with Pistoclerus, but then the play continued, with friendship restored and a second deception. Here, then, is a good example from Menander and Plautus of a brief and casual employment of the type which, I suggest, receives its most elaborate development, at least in surviving material, from Philemon and Plautus.

To expand upon the illustration from the *Bacchides* and sketch out a general typology, we might start from the basic need for help: that is, regularly, for assistance in a love affair. One young man has fallen in love with a courtesan, and he needs various kinds of support from a buddy (*sodalis*). The most basic support is simply money, since the ideal arrangement is to buy the courtesan free from her pimp-owner, and the young lover almost never has the necessary purchase price. Rarely, as in the *Pseudolus*, the friend (Charinus) readily provides the needed sum; more commonly, the friend has as little available money as the lover, and so the lover must resort to alternative helpers or strategies. Besides money, the lover sometimes calls upon his friend to locate his beloved in her new residence in Athens or to try to track her down when she has disappeared with a rival, and he hopes for assistance in efforts to trick a pimp into a fake 'sale' or in other devices to gain possession of the girl. And sometimes he asks the friend to lend him the use of his house as a convenient love-nest.

A number of influences converged in the late fourth and early third centuries to make the helpful friend a popular character type that fitted superbly into the ethos of Greek New Comedy. The archetype of such friendships, that of Patroklos and Achilles in the *Iliad*, showed the way for later Greek tragedy to explore the pathos of self-sacrifice and the guilt in allowing another to take on one's own fatal danger. It was one of the great achievements of Euripides, in *Iphigenia in Tauris*, to represent the relationship between Orestes and Pylades as a moving competition in selflessness, total dedication to the service of the other. As a major influence on the melodramatic situations and characters of New Comedy, Euripides inevitably attracted attention to his sentimental pair of friends, ready to die for each other, both on the verge of sacrifice, then miraculously saved at the last moment. With appropriate adaptations, here was an ideal plot for New Comedy. During the fourth century, too, the story of Damon and Phintias gained currency. Damon took the place of Phintias, who had been condemned to death by Dionysios the Younger of Sicily in the late 360s – Philemon may have been born in Sicily in those very years – and Phintias, who had promised to return in time for the date of the execution, his own death, was unavoidably detained and, of course, nearly caused Damon, who was willing, to die in his place.[5] The shaping of this story and its wide circulation during subsequent decades testify to its resonance for Greek, and later Roman, emotions.

Another major development of the age, which thoroughly influenced New Comedy and certainly opened the eyes of dramatists and audience to the helpful friend, was the ethical inquiry into the nature of friendship which the various schools of philosophy rigorously pursued. Philemon had already embarked on his career as a comic playwright when Aristotle produced the sections of his *Ethics* on friendship.[6] Aristotle's successor, Theophrastos – said to have been a teacher of Menander – devoted a special treatise (now lost) to a new examination of the subject. Epicurus, a friend and contemporary of Menander, preached and practised a model form of friendship. Aristotle and Epicurus, and presumably other writers on the question, focused much attention on the proper motivation of friendship – whether utility, pleasure, or virtue. In an ideal conception, the ethical writers agreed, pleasure results from friendship, and helpfulness constitutes a regular concomitant, but neither should be the primary motive for forming such a relationship because neither can supply the main constituent – selfless mutual concern or virtue. Those who seek their own pleasure and profit from friendship soon find that friendship does not exist for them. As Cicero formulated it in his little treatise about friendship (which mythologized the relationship of Laelius and Scipio), 'Friendship has not, therefore, resulted from personal advantage, but personal advantage has resulted from friendship' (*non igitur utilitatem amicitia, sed utilitas amicitiam secuta est*).[7] To apply this doctrine to the comic type of helpful friend: the *sodalis* demonstrates his friendship by his willingness to serve the lover's desperate and often intemperate needs and demands; but the lover often exposes his somewhat comic limitations – and, thereby, the comic qualities of his love – by pressing unreasonable demands on and voicing unfair accusations of his chum's helpfulness. Thus, the lover often reveals a deficiency of virtue in friendship, which also applies to other areas of his life, namely, love and family responsibility.

It is impossible to determine the date and order of Philemon's plays, but we can securely place Plautus' *Mercator*, adapted from Philemon's *Emporos*, close to 200 BC (because of its small amount of lyric, its modest adventure into rollicking comedy of action and speech, and its particularly coherent plot), a decade or more before the Roman produced *Trinummus*, his evidently freer adaptation of *Thensauros*. I shall then begin with *Mercator*, because, being more faithful to Philemon, it preserves the fullest and most impressive role for the helpful friend that has survived from antiquity.

Eutychus, the friend who is rapidly pressed into service and proves capable, eventually, of saving the day for the young and desperate lover Charinus, makes his first appearance towards the end of what would have been Act II in Philemon's play. We have seen Charinus' crisis steadily developing. Sent off by his strict father to trade across the Aegean, in order to escape the powerful lure of an Athenian courtesan, Charinus has done good business, but he has also fallen in love with a courtesan on Rhodes, bought her for himself, and brought her back with the intention of smuggling her into his home as a 'servant' for his mother. Hardly has he arrived in port at Piraeus and started worrying about the deception he has plotted against his father, than the father, visiting the ship and spotting the gorgeous 'servant,' rapidly sheds his mask of austerity and starts to plot how he himself can get possession of the girl for some erotic pleasures in his advanced age. Thus, son and father each lust for the same girl, each ignorant of the other's desires and plans, each guilty of dishonesty but innocent of any intention of stealing the other's love. Philemon puts us squarely on the side of Charinus, the son, because young love regularly takes priority over old lechery; because the father, Demipho, has a wife; and finally because Charinus has purchased the girl with his own hard-earned money, some of the profits from his trading expedition. Yet, in an opening encounter with Demipho, the trader-son quickly loses control of the girl. When the father invents an imaginary friend who will buy the girl – she is purportedly much too pretty to be a safe and reliable servant – all that Charinus can do is lamely invent a young man who will supposedly buy the girl for a better price. Since he believes his father and knows he himself is lying, Charinus capitulates helplessly when Demipho orders him to stay at home, then heads off to the port to make sure of his personal plans. As the desperate lover, full of self-pity, announces his intention to do away with himself, Eutychus, the friend, emerges from hiding to take on the role of helper.

As Eutychus himself states at line 477, he has heard the conversation between father and son, so he knows exactly what Charinus does, but less than we in the audience know (because we are privy to Demipho's erotic motivations). Recognizing the obvious need, he offers to go to the port himself, to act the part of the imaginary 'young purchaser' and beat Demipho to ownership of the beloved. He has identified himself as friend, chum, and nearest neighbour (tuos amicus et sodalis, simul vicinus proximus, line 475), and, in offering his services and accepting the details of his commission (mandatum, line 495), he moves into the familiar outlines of the helpful friend, Apuleius' sodalis opitulator. The act ends on this note of hope for Charinus.

Act III starts by quickly blasting that hope. First, we see the henchman of Demipho, who happens to be Eutychus' father, enter with the girl and escort her into his house, which is planned as Demipho's temporary 'love-nest.' Once the stage is empty, anxious Charinus appears, wondering where Eutychus is and whether he has succeeded in his mission.[8] In the distance, he spots a running figure, who proves to be Eutychus, with the customary bad news that messengers running from the port of Athens usually deliver. The girl has been bought before he got there, and, to his knowledge, she has simply disappeared with her unknown new owner. The wild lover reacts violently and ungratefully to the honest failure of his friend; he extravagantly accuses him of murder (because the loss of his love makes Charinus regularly turn to suicidal thoughts in his helplessness). In less metaphorical language, Charinus fixes on what he considers the betrayal of the 'trust' of their friendship (perdidisti me et fidem mecum tuam, line 625). Therefore, if Eutychus does not immediately locate the girl, the lover threatens to leave loveless and friendless Athens and depart for 'exile' (line 648). Charinus goes ranting off to say farewell to his parents, leaving Eutychus to consider how he can possibly redeem his failure, how he can find the girl without any clues, and how he can rescue himself from feeling responsible and being blamed for the departure of his pal. Act III ends, then, on a melodramatic note of seeming 'tragedy' for true friendship, to say nothing of love.

We know that the object of Eutychus' quest and of Charinus'

passion is right there behind them, inside Eutychus' home. When he turns away from his home and heads energetically to the forum to start an official search, we are intrigued. But justice starts to work for the young men in Act IV. Eutychus' mother comes home, discovers the girl, and naturally leaps to the conclusion that *her* husband (not Demipho) is conducting an illicit affair. That embroils Eutychus' father, but also leads to surprisingly happy 'bad news' for Eutychus, when he returns exhausted from his wild goose chase after the girl (lines 805 ff).

Philemon has set up – and Plautus respectfully uses – a very Hellenic, moral, sentimental, and socially edifying conclusion that features Eutychus as the dominant figure, helping all the fallible characters, old and young, to become reconciled and to return to useful, happy lives. As in Act II, he comes upon despairing Charinus (line 857), who is about to pursue the drastic decision of going into 'tragic' exile, like the character Teucer who, in myth, was banished from Greece and obliged to sail to a new home on Cyprus.[9] This time, however, Eutychus does control the situation and can, indeed, provide the necessary help. He takes Charinus inside to the missing girl. Then, he re-emerges from his home just as his father and Demipho anxiously rush on. After quickly greeting his father with the relieving news that the jealous wife has been mollifed (line 965), he turns to Demipho and demolishes his hopes, overwhelms him with guilt in relation to his son and with panic in connection with his wife, then smooths the whole situation over. It was enough to get the father's admission of remorse towards Charinus and to have frightened him with the threat of informing his wife. As the play's final speaker, Eutychus exhibits his dominance as helper when, sounding like a respected legislator, he declares a new 'law' against old lechers like Demipho and in favour of young lovers like Charinus (lines 1015 ff).

The helpful friend, by definition, could never be the principal character of a play, but Philemon and Plautus have given him the maximum prominence in the *Mercator*. The lover Charinus appears in four of the five acts; helpful Eutychus works with him and on his behalf in three acts, playing an ever more significant role until he comes to dominate the final act, as we have seen. It is apparent that Philemon presented helpfulness as an admirable trait and worked to give it increased sentimental appeal by plotting difficulties in the path of its success. Eutychus is not a comic personality, certainly not one who is allowed to stand away from his role and comment ironically on it; and we as audience sympathize with him and his selfless helpfulness. Taking over the character, Plautus does not tamper with its essential sentimental earnestness. What Plautus does is to weaken our sympathy towards Charinus, the object of all Eutychus' efforts, by making his love and despair ostentatiously histrionic. When he lets Charinus talk in a 'tragic' manner, comparing himself to Pentheus (lines 469 ff), then rush off to commit suicide, he does not so much invite us to feel concern for this foolish young man as to smile or, indeed, laugh at his extravagant behaviour. When Charinus overreacts to the news that Eutychus has missed buying the girl at the port and accuses his friend of a capital crime against himself (lines 611 ff), of outright treachery, that excess turns us against the excessively egotistic lover and in favour of the friend. The more Charinus rants, the more attractive Eutychus becomes in his tolerance and continued dedication to service. (No lover can talk this way to any other character in comedy, not even to his own slaves.) Finally, when Charinus starts to act out his tragic role and play the part of Teucer going into exile, sailing aimlessly across the imaginary Aegean in search of a new home (lines 921 ff), he emotes thus at the moment when we and Eutychus know that all his problems have, in fact, been solved. So he seems particularly ridiculous, in contrast to the real and deserved satisfaction that his friend is allowed to voice and feel in a service ably performed.

Whereas Philemon seems throughout his drama to have been intent on developing and exploiting ethically satisfying sentimentality, and so worked with considerable imagination to explore the situations where friendship is tested and found supremely loyal, altruistic, and helpful, in spite of the strains that a demanding lover can put on the relationship, Plautus found his comic sense increasingly alienated by such 'tear-jerking' situations. We can perhaps sense his restlessness, even in the *Mercator*, when he distances himself and the audience from the lover and implicitly stirs some questions about the reality of friendship between helpful Eutychus and such a foolish figure of complaint, accusation, and exaggerated behaviour as Charinus. However, at this early point in his career as playwright, he did not have anything to substitute, and no automatic devices for change, as he later did. Roughly ten years later, when he composed the *Trinummus*, he felt more self-confident in the face of Philemon's sentimentality, and so he intervened forcefully to alter it. The helpful friend had to yield to a more vigorous comic purpose, and soon he ceased to be a significant character in Plautus' repertoire.

The helpful friend of the *Trinummus*, Lysiteles, tries to extricate his buddy Lesbonicus from an especially painful situation, one in which Philemon's inclination for sentimentality outdid itself. Lesbonicus has been such a total wastrel, in the absence of his hard-working merchant father, that he has exhausted all ready cash and then had the nerve to sell the family house, in order to finance his folly. He has not even a steady love affair to make himself somewhat appealing to us: he has lavished money on a variety of faithless courtesans. Selling his house is, of course, an act that symbolizes his utter abandonment of the central values of New Comedy – home, family, and domestic responsibility. Only at this late moment, does Lesbonicus painfully recognize that he has failed in his duty towards his nubile sister, who must have a dowry in order to secure a marriage appropriate to the family's former status. Without any money, how can he marry her to a man of honour, family, and property, as she once had a right to expect? Lesbonicus is overcome with remorse, but helpless. This is the moment for the helpful friend to appear, as Philemon planned it.

Lysiteles has lived a life so far that is the total antithesis of Lesbonicus' folly. He has been a very good son, prudent, responsible, entirely obedient and respectful towards his father, a kind but conservative man; and he has watched Lesbonicus' self-indulgence with disapproval, learning from the failure of his chum that it is better for a young man to pursue practical profit. Now, as Plautus presents the situation, Lysiteles suddenly sees how to help his buddy, even at the risk of considerable trouble with his own father: he will offer to marry Lesbonicus' sister without dowry, thus guaranteeing her an honourable and prestigious matrimony and freeing Lesbonicus from his helpless sense of guilt. Plautus prevents him from expressing any words of romantic interest in the girl, so that his motivation becomes so 'good' as to be preposterous.[10] And then the issue becomes one of perceiving the implications of this act of pure friendship, what Lysiteles considers *beneficium* – a simple good deed – in all its ramifications. We never see the girl involved, or hear anything about her. It is here, in the simplification of Lysiteles' motivations and character, I believe, that Plautus first intervened to attenuate the rich sentimentality that Philemon presumably sought from a fuller development of this situation, namely, as a combination of friendly helpfulness to Lesbonicus and satisfaction of genuine amatory interest on the part of Lysiteles. Marrying the sister constitutes, then, a congenial blending of two appealing desires, which together Lysiteles hopes to persuade his father to accept – and does – and confidently anticipates that Lesbonicus will welcome – but there he encounters firm opposition, to his and our surprise.

At this final moment, Lesbonicus has suddenly been struck with a sense of ethical propriety, and, no matter what Lysiteles wants to do for him and his sister, Lesbonicus can see only the disgrace to himself if he allows his sister to be wed without the customary dowry. What Lysiteles has proffered as *beneficium* earns a fierce rejection as *iniuria* (line 630). Regardless of what, in fact, is the situation of friendship with Lysiteles and the friend's obvious feeling of respect (and love, I add) for the sister, Lesbonicus grasps only the fact that marriage without dowry customarily means loss of status for the wife-to-be, so that she becomes more like a concubine than a wife and loses her claim to equality with her husband.[11] Intent on avoiding the reputation of having sacrificed his sister to such a fate, he then insists on finishing his own impoverishment by selling off his final piece of property for dowry, then setting off into self-imposed exile as a mercenary soldier. Lysiteles, in turn, cannot accept such a sacrifice and the disgrace it would cause him to be thought to have, in marrying Lesbonicus' sister, insisted on the total ruin of his best friend.[12] Plautus found this competition in self-sacrifice, a parody of the competition of Orestes and Pylades as to who would die, entirely satisfactory for his comic purposes and so eliminated the added amatory factor. But it was precisely the amatory factor in Lysiteles and the matching affection in Lesbonicus for the nameless sister that gave Philemon's situation its compelling sentimentality. When each of the young men threatened to break off the prospective marriage because of his sense of honour, of *beneficium* and *virtus*, he did it with great pain, not only because of the bond of friendship but also because of his feelings for the girl, and Lysiteles' pain would be especially evident.

Philemon's organization of the plot for this play was very different from that he employed in his *Emporos* (*Mercator*). Whereas in that play the interaction of the two friends (and hence the role of the *sodalis opitulator*) constituted the main interest, here the two friends have only one big scene together, in Act III, ending in an impasse of stubborn honour and embittered friendship; around that scene, a great deal of energetic effort is taken by other characters, including a set of helpful codgers of the older generation who try to promote the interests of Lesbonicus' father, which we can see are the long-range interests of Lesbonicus himself, if ever he recovers his responsibility and turns his back on the self-indulgent extravagances of recent years. Young Lysiteles has shot his bolt in offering to marry the sister without dowry; the angry refusal of proud Lesbonicus so irritates him that he threatens to end the friendship. Frustrated attempts to be helpful, and childish accusation from his pal do not stimulate him, as they did Eutychus, to try harder and eventually find the key to success; on the contrary, Lysiteles gives up and stalks off in fury (line 716). One of the older men, Callicles, has already purchased the home Lesbonicus rashly put up for sale, to secure it until the return of the father from his merchant voyage, but especially to keep control of some treasure the father buried in the house and asked Callicles to protect for use in a crisis (such as the wedding of the daughter). Now, Callicles, who recognizes the *flagitium* (line 612), like Lesbonicus, in marrying the girl off without dowry, decides to use some of the treasure towards a proper dowry.

Callicles finds himself in a bind, however. He does not trust

Lesbonicus, with reason, and so cannot reveal the existence of the treasure; if he did, he would expect Lesbonicus to waste it all in short order and leave the sister, undowered, worse off than ever. With an energetic inventiveness that puts helpful Lysiteles and helpless Lesbonicus to shame, he and another old friend devise a clever bit of trickery: they will hire a rogue to play the role of a messenger from the Orient, to announce money sent supposedly by Lesbonicus' father (but, in fact, taken from the treasure). That money will be dug up by Callicles, who in turn will use it for the girl's dowry – and all will be well. The lively old men really look forward to this flirtation with roguery.[13]

Act IV functions as the turning-point in the plot, in usual fashion, but not as the old 'rogues' have planned things. The hired 'Oriental' messenger arrives at the house, all right, but before he can carry out his task, Charmides, the father of Lesbonicus, who has just arrived at his (former) house, too, intervenes. Old Charmides proves to be the greatest rogue of all, though he acts with an entirely disinterested purpose, just to have fun and to top the obvious roguery of this man who claims to Charmides' face to be his personal emissary and intimate friend (line 895). Just as Plautus' *Bacchides* took its name from the special emphasis of the final scene, where the courtesans replaced the double-deceiver slave as the dominant characters and principal rogues, so Philemon's title, *The Treasure*, was replaced by *Trinummus* because of the lively scene of roguery and counter-roguery that Plautus here developed between Charmides and the inexpensive hireling – *Trinummus*' refers to the three coins he earned for his job. Having played his game with the imposter, Charmides remains in control of the field, but he still does not know what has happened. However, the clever but loyal servant of the family, Stasimus, appears providentially and informs him of enough details so that he can press quickly towards Plautus' conclusion. Plautus has built up the roguery of Act IV in order to free his play of the heavy sentimentality of Philemon's original, and, having once won his freedom, he has no intention of going back to do justice to those 'tear-jerking' themes.

What is left of Philemon's Act V, a mere seventy lines, winds things up in a most perfunctory manner. Plautus brings Lysiteles on with five lines of anapaestic lyric, much too short to be convincing, in which he sounds the theme of joy (*gaudium*, lines 1116 and 1119), without referring his happiness, as Eutychus did, to any specific thing, either to his own love or to his friendship. Encountering Charmides, he quickly secures approval of his plan to marry the daughter, but now *with* a dowry, as Charmides can easily insist. Then, he perfunctorily intercedes on behalf of Lesbonicus, so that the father forgives his son. In effect, then, without either young man having done anything himself, their impasse has been dissipated. The wedding on honourable terms has been determined; the love of Lysiteles for the girl is about to be gratified; and the basic friendship of the two young men can now be renewed. Lysiteles has performed a slight service in speaking up for Lesbonicus, and now he happily calls his chum out to meet his affectionate father. When Lesbonicus, still unaware of the happiness that awaits him, still in his stubborn mood, surlily asks who it is that summons him with so much racket, Lysiteles answers, 'It is your well-wisher and friend' (*benevolens tuos atque amicust*, line 1177). That is the only concession that Plautus will allow to the lovingly developed theme of friendship and the painful strains on helpful Lysiteles, which Philemon had started in Act III and surely would have given its full due in his Act V. Plautus has gone along with sentimentality only so far, then altered the direction of the drama, changing its theme and tone, and thus ending with a comedy after his own and his audience's tastes, where the helpful friend has no significant function. Spirited old men are much more comically interesting, for Plautus, than young men who are engaged in highly delicate and sensitive ethical issues, but become immobilized by their problems and incapable of the vigorous speech and action that Plautus increasingly required in his truly comic roles.

We have seen how Plautus deconstructed the domestic themes of Menander in the *Bacchides*. Now, in the ethically complex and sentimentally satisfying situation of helpless and helpful friends, which Philemon explored with considerable versatility, we have an opportunity to observe Plautus at an early phase accepting unfunny sentiment, at a more mature stage deconstructing it with obvious gusto. Whether or not the *Mostellaria* was adapted from Philemon, it is tempting to regard this play as a very self-conscious improvement on the Greek's view of comedy. It starts with a repentant wastrel-lover (like Lesbonicus) and a loyal chum. But the *sodalis* is too drunk to be able to stand, let alone offer any help when the father suddenly comes home; and it is the intrepid slave Tranio who steps into the breech, takes charge (like a patron, a senator, and a general on campaign), to delay the moment of truth and to transfer the father's wrath from the son to himself at the end. It is this diversion, apparently, this abandonment of Philemon's plot and themes for the massive trickery of the rogue-slave which inspires the confident boast of Plautus at the end, through the mouth of Tranio, that he could teach the Greeks, both Philemon and Diphilos, something they sorely lacked: *optimas frustrationes* – the best ways to work out plots where rogues make fools of others. Now that we have seen how he felt obliged to minimize and replace Philemon's helpful friend, we can turn to what may be inferred about his self-confident deconstruction of Diphilos.

Diphilos' Big Scenes:
Plautus' Byplay with Melodrama

Plautus adapted two plays that are specifically credited to Diphilos, *Rudens* and *Casina*, and possibly a third, the now-tattered *Vidularia*. All three featured animated scenes of argument and decision, two by arbitration of a supposed outsider, the other by the process of drawing lots. By attempting to reconstruct these scenes in Diphilos, then comparing what Plautus made of the same situation, we have an opportunity to see how the Roman operated to heighten his sense of comedy in stage action and word. I shall concentrate on the known and complete adaptations – the earlier *Rudens*, and *Casina*, Plautus' last play.

In what would have been the Act IV of the first (of which we do not know the Greek title), Diphilos staged an angry dispute between two slaves over the trunk that one of them, Gripus, had fished out of the sea and the other, Trachalio, believes he recognizes as a key possession of his master's beloved, which she has lost in a shipwreck the previous night. Gripus imagines that the trunk contains vast quantities of wealth, which will enable him to secure his freedom and became a powerful Hellenistic ruler.[14] Trachalio, in contrast, suspects that the contents will be the baby trinkets of the girl, by which some day she may identify her parents and so regain the freedom to which she was born (before being kidnapped). The argument between the two slaves flares into hostile action; Trachalio seizes a rope that dangles from the trunk and tries to pull the booty out of the tight grasp of Gripus, and a comic tug-of-war ensues.[15] But when neither can prevail by strength, insults, or threats, both agree to abide by the decision of an arbiter. Gripus here plays cagy and pretends he doesn't know anybody in the neighbourhood (although, in fact, he is only a few steps from the property of his master, Daemones), and so Trachalio falls into his trap and agrees to ask Daemones to serve as arbiter. With supreme confidence, then, Gripus enters the arbitration process, sure that his master will be biased in his favour against this impudent stranger. Little does he know that Trachalio also has made the acquaintance of Daemones and can expect friendly treatment himself.

Daemones agrees to be the arbiter, and the slaves start to clamour for attention, each wanting his story to be heard first. When, to Gripus' shock and indignation, Daemones allows the 'stranger' Trachalio to have his say, Trachalio briefly outlines an appealingly altruistic case for allowing the girl, Palaestra, who he believes can identify the contents of the trunk as hers, to have her chance to prove her ownership once and for all (lines 1100 ff). This different motivation from the obvious greed of Gripus impresses the moral Daemones, and he orders Trachalio to fetch Palaestra for the test.[16] When she appears, the triangle of characters and interrelationships changes sharply, against the interests of Gripus, who increasingly becomes a voice of bitter protest and sardonic alienation. And what started off as an arbitration to determine the ownership of a trunk and its contents changes into a recognition scene, as Palaestra, in identifying the trinkets inside the trunk by fond memory, identifies herself to the arbiter as his long-lost daughter. Upright Daemones, who has been trying to be fair to his own slave and another, and to be dispassionate about the girl's claim to the contents of the trunk, necessarily lets his objectivity be undermined and welcomes the role of father that he thought he had lost forever. At the end of their happy recognition, father and daughter go indoors to find the mother, and Gripus, left alone, surlily meditates on his bad luck and contemplates, at least briefly, hanging himself.[17]

Diphilos has put together a masterful melodramatic turning-point for his play. He has embroiled two very different slaves in a dispute that builds into its melodrama elements of humour. Thanks to Gripus and his crass motivation and his understandably simple sense of possession – based on the old doctrine of finders keepers – Diphilos had a voice of angry outrage that we in the audience could laugh at and reject, because Gripus was so purely materialistic and impervious to the altruism and pathos of the others. The move from squabbling slaves to father and daughter was elegant, from Arbitration to Recognition: all the playwright did was to replace Trachalio (her agent) with Palaestra, and he shifted the direction of the scene from the largely comic slaves' dispute to the melodramatic identification of the trinkets, which amounted to self-identification of Palaestra, with the result that Daemones was pulled into close relationship and Gripus was simultaneously expelled. This act shows how brilliantly Diphilos could handle the limitation on three speaking parts, how ably he could modulate from more obvious comedy to melodrama, yet always kept a down-to-earth Gripus on hand, to prevent the melodrama from becoming too sentimental.

It is generally believed that New Comedy derived this melodramatic situation from Euripidean melodrama. Hyginus 181 preserves for us a story about Alope, which is thought to go back to Euripides himself or to one of his imitators. Neptune raped Alope, who of course became pregnant. Afraid of her father's rage, she had the baby exposed as soon as it was born, wrapping it in one of her royal robes. A shepherd rescued it and gave it to a friend, who desperately wanted a baby for his childless wife. The first shepherd kept the rich robe for his troubles, and, when the second began to demand that, too, as the rightful possession of the baby, their argument required an arbiter. They went to their royal master, who quickly recognized the robe as his daughter's and thus realized that the baby was his illegitimate grandson. In accord with the tragic pattern of response to Recognition, the king sentenced his innocent daughter to death and decreed that the baby should once more be exposed – this time, he hoped, more effectively. In this tragic plot, we find the main elements of Diphilos' comic situation: 1 / two servants wrangling over an item of value that goes with a foundling; 2 / their appeal to an arbiter (whom they may or may not know in some respect); 3 / the most important connection of the arbitrer with the issue emerges only during the arbitration, for it turns out that he is the baby's (foundling's) grandfather; 4 / thus, the arbitration leads directly to a recognition.

Diphilos used all those elements of the tragic plot, with one variation that enriched his melodrama considerably: instead of making the foundling a newborn baby, pathetically dependent on others to defend its interests, he created a pathetic but very articulate woman to take part in the recognition. Hence, Act IV is divided into two separate phases, and Trachalio, the foundling's loyal spokesman in the initial phases of arbitration, is replaced with Palaestra herself when the decisive phase arrives. By good luck, papyrus recovery has spared us a major arbitration scene, from Menander, and a fortunate mosaic illustration indicates what the audience actually saw on stage, so that we can compare how another Greek writer treated the same material.

Menander's play was named after the brilliant scene he devised – hence, *The Arbitrants (Epitrepontes)*. Here, we find the basic elements in this form: 1 / Two shepherds enter, arguing over the ownership of some baby trinkets, whether or not they belong to a baby one has found and given to the other, without the trinkets. 2 / Unable to resolve the matter, they appeal to an older man as he emerges from his house. The man does not know either of them, angrily tries to brush them off, but finally agrees to act as arbiter. 3 / In fact, though, he is the baby's grandfather, and we probably know this detail from a divine prologue, even if all the characters act in ignorance. 4 / Menander does not directly connect the arbitration with a recognition; the decision of the arbiter leads to no immediate clarification, but it indirectly starts the intricate process by which eventually the baby is identified – first, by family adherents; then, by the parents; and, finally, by the grandfather who had earlier been the arbiter. Thus, Menander's ingenious innovation was to separate Arbitration from Recognition, to place the arbitration in Act II, and to develop it independently. When he finished with it, he also had no further use for the shepherd-disputants, and they drop out. He maintained our interest in the chief trinket, a ring, showing how it led to the baby's father, and eventually to the mother, too; how an act of drunken human rape could be alleviated by repentance; how the baby could finally be the foundation of a marriage that even the choleric grandfather (the earlier arbiter) could welcome. What in tragedy was unacceptable and led to death, in comedy can be transmuted into happiness. That gap that Menander forces between Arbitration in Act II and the separate stages of Recognition in Acts IV and V emphasizes the different functions and ethical imports of what, in Alope and Diphilos, are two phases of a complex single act, the turning-point of the play.

Greek comedy adhered to a convention that limited speaking characters to three in any single scene, and so Menander's text clearly indicates that the speakers consist of the two arguing rustics and old Smikrines (the unknown grandfather). But a mosaic, which illustrates this, the most famous scene and source of the name of the play, proves that Menander had more than three persons on stage in front of the audience.[18] There were two silent extras: the wife of the shepherd Daos and the baby, for whom she and Daos claim to be acting, whose fate, of course, is thereby visually connected with the response of Smikrines. Menander thus reminds us of the principal goal of all this anxious arbitration and points forward to the eventual recognition that will restore the baby to its home. And by increasing the number of characters on stage, he tends to add importance and action to an already lively scene.

It does not appear that Diphilos used more than three speakers and characters on stage in each of the two parts of his act that combined Arbitration and Recognition. However, by taking the slave Trachalio off and replacing him with the interested foundling Palaestra, he did necessarily enlarge the scope of the scene and alter its tone. Fierce argument and threats dominate the confrontation, all of which the Greek staged, between the two slaves that leads up to the arbitration. Immediately after Daemones has begun to arbitrate and Trachalio has secured a role for Palaestra over the shrill protests of Gripus, Trachalio leaves to get the girl; and, when she enters, the main discussion and action increasingly involve her with Daemones, while Gripus, progressively ignored, can only helplessly comment with bitter asides. Diphilos intentionally differentiated Trachalio and the girl: the slave appears to be clever, dedicated, quite masculine enough to face up to the threats of the fisherman Gripus and hold his own physically, whereas she plays the innocent, honest, trusting young girl, naïvely involved in her own past and her long search for her parents, almost unaware of what happens around her.

It is undoubtedly significant that Plautus' comedy became entitled *Rudens, The Rope*. That rope dangles from the chest that Gripus proudly lugs on at the opening of this scene, and Trachalio, who follows him on in short order, grabs hold of the rope, starts to pull on it in order to hold Gripus still and get his attention, and as a result a kind of tug-of-war ensues, Gripus trying to break away with his spoil, about which he has glorious dreams, and Trachalio trying to keep the chest under some control until, if possible, their dispute can be decided by arbitration. The title implies that this scene, not the recognition or arbitration itself, was the most brilliant comic portion of the play. Although we do not know Diphilos' title and therefore cannot claim that Plautus' represents a significant change of emphasis, Plautus' text does contain clear evidence of his efforts to elaborate his comic opportunities.

Consider the following points: 1 / Plautus' Act IV extends to roughly four hundred lines, that is, about one hundred lines more than the longest acts that have survived from Menander. We can probably assume that Diphilos' comedies, contemporary and competitive with Menander's and Philemon's, had much the same proportions, namely, five acts, for a total of just under a thousand lines. 2 / Plautus gives Gripus an entrance monody of more than thirty lines. Not only are the lyric metres entirely Plautine embellishment, a skilful and delightful combination of boastful bacchiacs and incredibly confident anapaests, but the speech, unrealistically long for a character at this point in the play, consists of familiar Plautine verbal routines. 3 / Plautus develops the tug-of-war scene between the slaves, Gripus and Trachalio, over a hundred lines before Gripus agrees to resort to an arbiter (lines 938–1040). This development is justified by the comic potential of wildly arguing, threatening slaves on stage; it is not warranted by the plot, which looks to Arbitration and Recognition, as we saw. (Menander does not let his rustics act out their hostility; he obliges them to explicate it verbally to the arbiter and us in the audience.) The tug-of-war itself was no doubt in Diphilos, but Plautus has prolonged it by expanding the dialogue here. The two slaves get to arguing about the 'law of the seas,' which can, of course, be applied sensibly to something found in the water, but lost in shipwreck. However, the argument becomes sidetracked and focused on a non-legal, obviously comic issue, namely, whether a chest fished from the sea can be considered to be a 'fish.' That is, I believe, one extensive Plautine addition. Another would be a short anapaestic anecdote assigned to Trachalio (lines 955 ff), entertaining but never put to any use. 4 / Once Daemones appears (lines 1045 ff) and becomes the arbiter – Plautus cuts out almost entirely the normally necessary negotiations by which a man agrees to be arbiter and sets some rules about his authority – the slaves now proceed to argue at length before him (lines 1060–1128). The plot requires that some discussion take place, so that Daemones will agree to open the chest and test Palaestra's memory of its contents, but most readers can find signs of Plautus' workmanship in some of the repetitions and Latinate puns and alliteration.

5 / Whereas, then, Plautus' text shows that he devotes more than 220 lines to various stages of the highly entertaining argument between the two slaves, to the recognition he is content to give only 50 lines (lines 1129–75). I believe that those proportions reveal the relative emphasis of the Roman writer, who has skewed the greater balance of Diphilos' drama and thus performed his now-predictable deconstruction of Greek melodrama. The reunion

and family reintegration are not the goal of Plautine comedy. However, it must be admitted that Plautus did see reason to enlarge the theatrical impressiveness of the recognition scene by adding two characters to Diphilos' three. He does not remove Trachalio, and, besides Palaestra, he employs her friend Ampelisca. In Roman comedy, as we have noted, a playwright can utilize more than three speakers at a time, so Trachalio on stage remains perfectly articulate. Thus, he can continue the byplay with Gripus that Diphilos decisively ended before the recognition, but Plautus has already considerably expanded earlier and apparently now finds too appealing to abandon. At line 1175, Palaestra finally looks up from her preoccupation with the trinkets in the chest to find herself being embraced and hailed as daughter by this old man who has been acting as arbiter. She briefly is allowed to say: 'Hail, father I had given up hoping to find' (*salve, mi pater insperate*), and the text permits her no more words about her feelings, her past experiences, or her concern for her lover. Plautus quickly gets this saccharine subject off stage and proceeds with more obvious comedy.

We do not have so much useful comparative material to help us analyse Diphilos' and Plautus' respective achievements in Act II of the play, which later Romans called *Casina*, but which in fact may have been known by the title *Sortientes*, a close translation of Diphilos' title and a probable indication that Plautus, as well as the Greek playwright, put his brilliant comic imagination to work on the staging of the lot-drawing scene. Euripides offered a tragic model in his *Aiolos*, where King Aeolus decided to marry his sons to his daughters and assign the couples by lot. Since one son and daughter were already linked by incestuous passion, when the lot failed to match them, the son committed suicide. But Diphilos left that tragic model, if he was conscious of it, far behind.

Drawing lots was a common method of deciding issues, serious as well as trivial, in the ancient world. Ideally affected by pure luck, lots could be managed in various ways. At lines 398–9, Olympio refers to the myth of a notoriously corrupt lot drawing that benefited Cresphontes.[19] Diphilos placed his scene in Act II, which means that he made it part of the plot complication.

He did this by arranging it so that the lot came out in favour of the obviously wrong person, and the rest of the comedy had to correct that injustice; where fate had bungled, enterprising human beings had to act energetically, and successfully, to reverse the situation and punish the comic 'villains.' As with the comic arguments which we have been studying, this dispute flares between two slaves, in the same household: Olympio, the caretaker of the rural estate, and Chalinus, the sturdy attendant of the young master in Athens and, when necessary, on campaign.[20] However, behind the two slaves lurks a bitter controversy between the old master, Lysidamus, and his wife, Cleustrata. The slaves are going through a charade of competition to possess and marry Casina, a young girl who has the status of household slave (though she really, we know, belongs mysteriously to a 'good family,' having been exposed at birth by her mother and found, the conventional background to a recognition in comedies). In fact, Lysidamus has put Olympio up as a front, so that he can satisfy his shameful lust on the maid without his wife's knowledge. But Cleustrata herself wants to control the disposition of her personal maid and favours the cause of Chalinus, who is acting as a front for the dubious desires of the young master (not present during the play). At the start, though Plautus somewhat confuses us on this point, Diphilos may have represented Cleustrata as ignorant of both husband's and son's purposes, believing, that is, the lies of Olympio and Lysidamus that both were passionately seeking a normal marriage for the rustic, and nothing else.

The surface comedy in the dispute – threats, insults, and much comic anger – closely resembles what Diphilos does as he portrays the tug-of-war between Gripus and Trachalio in the original of *Rudens*. But, whereas the dispute of *Rudens* masks the progress towards Recognition, this dispute conceals a guilty comic amour of a lecherous old husband. Olympio talks and acts confidently and menacingly, because he knows that he has the master on his side; Chalinus stands up to his threats, but he has little but right on his side, no matter what Cleustrata does. And she probably does little, in Diphilos, until after the lot drawing. Only then do Chalinus and she discover the real purposes of Lysidamus and start to conspire to frustrate him.

Diphilos' lot-drawing scene was undoubtedly a brilliant conception and wonderful melodrama. It featured the three men, with Lysidamus presiding over the drawing of lots from a bucket of water where they floated. Each of the lots was marked, and, to ensure 'fairness,' neither Olympio nor Chalinus was permitted to draw, but the supposedly 'impartial' Lysidamus would have pulled one lot, which would then identify the husband-to-be of Casina. Diphilos gave the two slaves a spirited dialogue, in which each accuses the other of cheating, threatens and probably gives blows, prays ludicrously for fulfilment of his corrupt desires, and keeps appealing to the master for help against the other. Whether Lysidamus actually cheated, as frequently happens in lot drawing, or was a beneficiary of unfair luck, the lot that came out was Olympio's. So Olympio and Lysidamus, both alike feeling victorious, went off to make preparations for the wedding and its banquet, while Chalinus, left alone, voiced his frustration and contemplated hanging himself (lines 424 ff).

What Plautus does is to enlarge the scene and its interrelationships by adding Cleustrata as a fourth speaking character. Although, as a mere wife, with no financial power over Lysidamus, she technically can exert no influence on the ceremony or its results and, in Diphilos, knew nothing of Lysidamus' perverse intentions with Casina and this 'marriage,' and accordingly was unnecessary at the lot drawing, Plautus has determined to build up her role throughout the comedy; and he deliberately includes her in this scene so that we continuously sense the antagonism between husband and wife that lies behind the verbal abuse and exchange of blows of the obviously hostile slaves.

Chalinus appears, carrying the bucket and lots, and behind him follows Cleustrata (lines 353 ff). 'What does my husband want of me?' she asks. 'To see you dead,' replies Chalinus. That is part of an obvious Plautine misogynistic routine and sets the comic tone and basic theme of Plautus' adaptation. After some crude comments exchanged by the slaves, Plautus has Lysidamus address his wife as follows (lines 364 ff): 'I thought that I could gain my request of you, my wife, that Casina be given as wife to me.' She angrily replies: 'Given to *you*?' And Lysidamus begins to stumble and stutter, as he realizes that he has betrayed himself to her. Whereas Diphilos prevented Cleustrata from suspecting anything until after the lot fell in favour of Olympio (and Lysidamus), Plautus exploits her added presence in this scene to make the guilt and embarrassment of the lecherous husband comically obvious from the start. Cleustrata continues to remain adamantly against the marriage with Olympio, and that forces Lysidamus to risk the uncertainty of the lots. Plautus returns to the text of Diphilos, and more angry, sneering exchanges between the slaves, who anxiously await the drawing of the lucky lot. Then, he figures out another dramatic function for the wife: to ensure the appearance of fairness, Lysidamus, with a big show of magnanimity, invites her to draw the lots (lines 393–5). More bitter argument from the slaves leads to each being authorized, by master, then mistress, to slug the other. Finally, at line 412, Lysidamus urges his wife to draw and commands the slaves to pay attention. He himself expresses his own anxiety over the result. She puts her hand into the pail and pulls out a lot, and, to the surprise of us in the audience, the dismay of Chalinus and Cleustrata, and the absolute delight of Olympio and Lysidamus, it turns out that the lot is Olympio's. Lysidamus, therefore, sends his wife off, and she voices her obedience, to prepare the wedding (lines 419 ff).

By expanding the scene of Diphilos, who, restricted to three speakers, kept our attention on the way Lysidamus organized and managed the charade of lot drawing and secured for himself an unjust result that guaranteed his lust's satisfaction, Plautus put on stage and gave an effective voice to all four characters who are affected by this lot. To Cleustrata, who in Diphilos had no knowledge of her husband's intentions, he assigned strong suspicions and even apparent knowledge of Lysidamus' passion for Casina, so that her opposition, from the beginning, is conscious and thematically significant:[21] she resists a home-breaker, a disrupter of her family, an irresponsible and extravagant fool. Her husband wishes her 'dead,' just as foolish sons in love wish their parents dead in Plautus, because the lover's impetus to irresponsibility wants to destroy all sensible opposition. It was a particularly felicitous touch of irony that Plautus achieved when he had Cleustrata draw the lot that would, at least briefly, bring her opposition to a jolting halt. Although this brilliant scene covers barely seventy lines, Plautus has diverted it skilfully to his kind of comedy, enhancing in advance the role of the wife, making her a vigorous, no-nonsense equal of her husband, not a tame victim of his plot, and he has balanced the loud words and vigorous gestures the slaves exchange with the more subtle antagonism of wife and husband, which taps the timeless themes of marital tension, the selfishness of the husband in this case, and the struggle for power in a home where the man will wreck the household to satisfy his lust, and the wife stands for the general needs of house and family, rather than her personal advantage.

Earlier in Act II, Plautus introduces us to Cleustrata, then to Lysidamus, and he devises for each of them a separate and emphatic scene of lyrics. Cleustrata gets a series of bacchiacs and cretics, in which she denounces her disgraceful old husband and expresses her determination not to cooperate with him in any way, but rather to harry him with words and to prevent him from enjoying the usual comforts of home, food, and drink (lines 144 ff). She knows, she claims, that he is pursuing his own selfish love, so she will make his life as miserable as he deserves, 'that food of death, pursuer of disgrace, den of iniquity' (*Accheruntis pabulum, flagiti persequentem, stabulum nequitiae*). The metre, the list of insults, the rhyming nouns at start and end – all show the handiwork of Plautus, verbal magician par excellence, and the whole effect of the introduction of the wife is to make her a powerful figure of comic antagonism to the husband, Lysidamus, who soon dances in, hideously dressed like a young lover, reeking of perfume, and trilling a love song (lines 217 ff). In a later chapter, I discuss in greater detail the ways in which Plautus develops the role of Cleustrata after the lot drawing and creates in her one of his most original comic heroines. For now, it is enough to see that he treated Diphilos' big title scene of lot drawing with full independence. It was a wonderfully uproarious scene, but it had only three males and an unequal part for Chalinus, who thus seems marked from the beginning for defeat. By adding Cleustrata, Plautus balanced the forces of antagonism and gave the lot taking a new aura of impartiality, which is then destroyed by the wilful unfairness of Fortune.

Momentarily checked and humbled, Cleustrata goes off to make the preparations she initially asserted she never would for disgraceful Lysidamus. But his victory and her defeat last barely a hundred lines. When Act III opens, she knows all, has made her campaign plans, and proceeds on a systematic counter-attack that ends by humiliating Olympio and Lysidamus, cleverly substituting brawny Chalinus as 'bride' in place of Casina and encouraging him to take full advantage of the 'privacy and trust of the marriage bed' to beat the unsuspecting 'lovers' mercilessly.

Plautus consciously invited his audience in the *Mostellaria* to compare his achievement with that of Philemon and Diphilos. 'If you're a friend of those Greeks,' he says, 'tell them how the servant has made a fool of his master, and you'll be supplying them with something they never had, the finest fooling.' In other plays, the invitation to compare is less ostentatious, but it is implicitly there. Accepting that implicit bidding, I have tried to demonstrate the comic techniques that appear in Plautus' adaptation of the helpful friend, a favourite character of Philemon's sentimental and sententious comedy. In an early play, before he has achieved his comic independence, the Roman does not risk himself in deconstruction; but, in the later *Trinummus*, the helpful friend and noble morality yield to the more vigorous verbal and theatrical humour of the now-mature Plautus. As we shall see, Plautus has realized that he does not want to feature rather obviously good helpers, like friends, but to delight us, in spite of the demands of plot realism and ethical propriety, with rogue-helpers, with a roguish father like Charmides, with a roguish slave like Tranio (whom Plautus apparently considered the epitome of his comic originality at the time).

Diphilos seems to have been less sentimental than Philemon and closer in spirit to Plautus than perhaps any of the known Greek writers whose works he adapts. Nevertheless, Plautus did feel independent. It is probable that Diphilos never achieved and perhaps never even essayed a plot that allowed a slave to turn a master into a fool. But we have concentrated on scenes where Diphilos did achieve striking success by staging raucous disputes between slaves and making them intersect with the different purposes of their masters, with Daemones' recognition of his daughter in the original of *Rudens*, with Lysidamus' lecherous pursuit of his housemaid in *Kleroumenoi*. In both his adaptations, Plautus availed himself of the greater flexibility of theatrical conventions in Rome to enlarge the cast and to make the comic clashes that much more obvious. In the earlier *Rudens*, he contents himself with sabotaging the melodrama of Recognition by overemphasizing the verbal and physical comedy of a slave dispute. In his final *Casina*, he shows a more mature comic independence as he employs the expanded lot drawing to fashion Cleustrata into a purely Plautine comic lead. 'If you're a friend of Diphilos,' he might then have said, 'tell him how I produced a "heroic" comic wife who made a fool rightly of her husband, something Diphilos never could do.'

CHAPTER THREE

Plautus' Plotting:
The Lover Upstaged

When classical scholars began to develop an interest in New Comedy, then to pursue that interest with fervour under the stimulus of the new papyrus finds of this century, they themselves were living in a period of sentimentality. Tastes in the Anglo-American cultures agreed with the romantic ideals of Victorian society, and parallel romanticism affected the judgment of other European classicists. Thus, it is common to find in general comments on New Comedy that the plot focused on love: 'The central theme was usually the course of true love, and the action depicted the efforts of a youth to obtain possession of his mistress, often in the face of the determined opposition of a parent or guardian, and with the assistance of a tricky slave.'[1] Even the diction of this sentence by Ashmore, which dates from 1910, sounds Victorian. Once it became conventional to treat New Comedy as romantic comedy, it also became easy to see how it anticipated the romantic plots of Renaissance, Italian, and Shakespearean comedy[2] and how it has continued to exert its influence on the romantic scenarios of Hollywood (especially of the 1930s and 1940s) and of the various so-called situation comedies (sitcoms) of postwar television.

Although I am suggesting that classical scholars, children of their own sentimental age, were predisposed to find and value romantic love plots in Greek New Comedy and to minimize the significance of exceptions, I hasten to add that earlier ages, also sentimentally inclined, made the same generalizations. It was a commonplace, for instance, that love was the 'breath of life' in

Menander's plays. Ovid said it in the first decade of the first century AD (as he defended his own use of love topics in his poetry): *fabula iucundi nulla est sine amore Menandri* ('No play of delightful Menander exists without love'). Later, in the same century, Plutarch, a great admirer of the Greek playwright, declared that in every play of Menander the breath of life comes from love. The sententious and sentimental Stobaeus cited Plutarch's comments with full approval in the sixth century.[3] Plutarch also commented with great admiration on the propriety of Menander's love plots. Menander always left his audiences with a good feeling about love, an optimism about marriage and the commitments of mutual affection.[4]

Plautus did not agree with Menander on this point, as on so many others, and in this chapter I review the ways in which he sabotaged the love plot and its amatory themes and upstaged the lover, determined not to write romantic comedy but Roman comedy with an emphasis on humour derived from intrigue, roguery, wit, and outright romantic parody. We can watch him taking the Menandrian originals, which centred their attention on the positive worth of love, and warping them into a new anti-romantic theme. The changes which he introduced in *The Double-Deceiver*, as he adapted it into the *Bacchides*, involved, among other things, denying the fathers the authority to control their sons' irresponsible love and instead subjecting them to the same irresponsible urges as their immature progeny. Plautus' final scene does not point towards responsible domestic love, but towards sexual promiscuity.[5]

The two fathers, Nicobulus and Philoxenus, storm up to the house of the courtesans where their two sons, they now know, are royally entertaining themselves with the money fraudulently gained from Nicobulus. When the two Bacchides open the door at their loud pounding, angry Nicobulus faces one, and the other makes Philoxenus, a milder and more impressionable old man, her target. As the women seductively tease the men, Philoxenus begins to melt. Here is the conversation of the two greybeards: Philoxenus: 'Do you see that one?' Nicobulus: 'Yes.' Philoxenus: 'That's a woman who's not bad.' Nicobulus: 'Damn it, she *is* bad, and you're a scoundrel.' Philoxenus: 'Why waste words?

I love her.' Nicobulus: 'You in love?' Philoxenus: 'Certainly' (spoken in ostentatious Greek, like French *mais oui*). Nicobulus: 'You decrepit human being, do you dare to become a lover at your age?' Philoxenus: 'Why not?' Plautus has let these characters bandy around the word for love – *amare* – as their theme, but the context makes a joke of Philoxenus' foolish infatuation. In the two different connotations of the word *mala* ('bad,' lines 1161–2), he produces a clever comic assessment of this love. Whereas Philoxenus ignores entirely the ethical nature of the courtesan and sees only her physical attractions and her pleasing manner, Nicobulus insists on her essential badness. But, as I have already noted and elaborate in a later chapter, a woman's badness (*malitia*) has special positive value in Plautus' world, and so, although Philoxenus is weak and ridiculous in 'loving' his Bacchis, he also strikes the Roman audience as thoroughly in line with the comic 'virtues' supported by Plautus: not romantic love, but sensual love that can be gratified by old and young alike.

Did Greek New Comedy Always Feature Romantic Love?

Before I examine the ways in which Plautus lets the lover be upstaged, it would be well to modify somewhat the seemingly stark opposition between what I have called the romantic love of Menander (and, by implication, of all Greek New Comedy) and the anti-romantic, Roman enjoyment of sensual love in Plautus. Although it may be convenient to attribute to the Greek writers of comedy a single sentimental attitude towards love, even our fragmentary acquaintance with Menander's main rivals obliges us to admit that they treated love differently. Whereas Menander built up plots where love meant a serious commitment and ultimately found deserved success in marriage and family, love breathed a different life in Philemon's and Diphilos' comedies.

Charinus of Philemon's *Emporos* (Plautus' *Merchant*) does not win the sympathy and interest of the audience in the way that Menander's lovers do.[6] He seems so helpless and so full of histrionic, 'tragical' self-pity, and his love, for a courtesan whom he has rashly bought, has no possibility of depth or long duration. In his opening soliloquy, he talks at length of all the faults (*vitia*) that accompany love (lines 18 ff). But this interminable and one-sided list is introduced by the statement that Charinus fell in love with a woman of outstanding loveliness while trading on Rhodes. Thus, his words about love's faults seem inconsistent with his confession of love: evidently, he does not really accept the fact that love amounts to a catalogue of negative qualities. But he has nothing very cogent to say about love on the positive side, and the woman he has suddenly become enamored with cannot offer him a lasting relationship such as those developed by Menander. Charinus will never be able to marry her, a foreigner and experienced prostitute. Nor does the love become any more valid when his foolish father suddenly abandons his strict principles and becomes Charinus' unknown rival. Philemon plots this love so as to create tensions between father and son, and between the two friends, and those tensions and resolutions constitute his primary interest: love is, in certain respects, only a comic gimmick.

Love occupies a still smaller part in the plot of Philemon's *Treasure* (Plautus' *Trinummus*), subordinate to the confusions of friendship between the two young men and the bumbling but well-meaning efforts of the older generation. Lesbonicus is no lover at all, and his friend Lysiteles seems to want to marry Lesbonicus' sister more out of friendship for Lesbonicus than for any affection for the girl (who is not allowed to appear on stage and impress the audience with the reality of this future wife). Like Charinus in *Emporos*, Lysiteles produces a soliloquy about love on his first entrance (lines 223 ff), and it also lays out the destructive, costly features of love. Lysiteles debates whether to commit his life to love or to practical advantage. As he slants it, there is no contest: Plautus makes him pun and say that love produces bitterness (*Amor amara dat tamen*, line 260), and that it will be no 'friend' of his (*Amor, mihi amicus ne fuas umquam*, line 267). Then, with an inconsequence that Plautus probably exaggerated, this same serious, practical, and reasonable young man suddenly proposes to his father (presumably the source of such wisdom on love) that he marry the dowerless sister of his chum Lesbonicus, merely as an act of friendship! We might think of this self-contradictory soliloquy on love's disadvantages, spoken by a young man who is taking on those admitted disadvantages, as a hallmark of Philemon and an indication of his special comic diminution of love and irrational lovers.[7]

Plautus, as we saw earlier, preserves the main lines of two comedies of Diphilos in his *Rudens* and *Casina*.[8] Neither makes significant use of romantic love. In the first, young Plesidippus does love the pseudo meretrix Palaestra, who eventually proves to be the long-lost daughter of Daemones and therefore marriageable. How little love contributes to plot and theme emerges clearly from the petty role of Plesidippus, the total lack of contact between the 'lovers' on stage, the absence of any words of love from either, and the careful attention devoted to other delightful details – namely, the wild behaviour and punishment of the pimp; the somewhat parodic Recognition; and all the comic excitement generated by the trunk, the rope, and the conflict of Gripus first with his fellow slave, then with the infamous pimp. If love is the breath of life for Menandrian comedy, for Diphilos it is a momentary gasp.

In the *Casina* (Diphilos' *Lot-Drawers*), young love has been removed from the play, so that the comedy can concentrate with raucous laughter on the crude lust of elderly Lysidamus, the witty obstruction and punishment contrived by the 'heroic' wife Cleustrata, and the rivalry between the slaves which Diphilos hilariously dramatizes in his inimitable scene of drawing lots. The Latin play now carries the name of the young girl who is the object of Lysidamus' lust (and supposedly of the honourable love of the absent son), but she never appears, and the title – which may replace Plautus' title, *Sortientes*, a translation of the Greek (line 32) – might well remind us of how far Diphilos has allowed himself to stray from the conventional romantic love-and-recognition plot. In short, Greek New Comedy does not present a standard attitude towards love: Menander tends to emphasize its humane qualities, both bad and good, and to plot his plays so that the lover earns a loving relationship by learning responsibility and commitment to family; Philemon isolates certain sententious views about love's disadvantages, then plays with somewhat foolish young and older lovers who nevertheless fall in love and cause complications that increasingly interest him;

Diphilos rather quickly marginalizes love, in order to free himself to use his broader sense of comedy on more obviously funny situations, especially the brawling of slaves, the beating of pimps, and even the physical humiliation of wayward masters.

Plautus and Love that Eventuates in Marriage

The standard romantic plot, of which Menander made himself supreme master and which Terence regularly employed after Plautus, takes marriage seriously and channels love towards that recognized social institution. Usually, an impetuous and irresponsible lover, in the course of the drama, comes to recognize his personal and social duties so that the love, which seemed doomed by his choice of female partner – courtesan (who in fact will locate her father and so become a legitimate choice for wife), virginal victim of his sexual assault, or virgin daughter in a family of slight financial means – becomes earned and worthy of ratification in marriage. We know of a few plots, too, that involve a young couple in their first year of marriage – such as Menander's *Arbitrants* and Terence's *Mother-in-Law* (adapted from an original by Apollodoros) – and in which an act of rape before marriage, which results in an early pregnancy after marriage, has to be dealt with. (The rape occurred under amazing conditions – drunkenness and darkness – so that neither rapist nor victim can recognize the other afterwards; and by sheer coincidence the rapist and his victim have married each other, in ignorant good faith on both parts. Since being married for these few months has brought genuine love, the plot works to preserve marriage, love, and the family, i.e., the new baby.)

Plautus does not favour plots that channel love into marriage, and even those that he adapts from his Greek sources he alters so that neither love nor marriage becomes the true goal of the action or the romantic end that his Roman audience desires. Only five of his twenty comedies proceed towards marriage (*Aulularia, Cistellaria, Curculio, Poenulus,* and *Rudens*).[9] Of these, only *Aulularia* involves a virgin who has been raped; the others portray the complications of a love that has been initiated with a courtesan who later proves to be the long-lost daughter of an Athenian, either kidnapped or abandoned as an infant, and, when 'recognized' during the play, capable of reintegration into legitimate society, and thus of happy marriage. Let us see what Plautus does with both these plot types and the ways in which he upstages the lover.

THE PREGNANT VIRGIN: *AULULARIA*

In comedies where the initial complication is rape by an impetuous lover, the girl never appears, and her voice is heard only once: when she cries out with labour pains (e.g., *Aulularia*, lines 691–2).[10] What love emerges, therefore, depends on the words and character of the young man and on the indirect description of others. Menander employed a significant device in *The Samian Woman* to introduce the lover and the serious quality of his commitment from the beginning: he had Moschion speak the prologue, explain the background, admit his rape, and sketch out the difficulties that were interfering with his determination to marry the girl and assume the role of father. In the *Aulularia*, a Household God delivers the prologue, and he concentrates on the miserly tradition of Euclio's family background. Euclio has a daughter who has proved to be a striking exception to the family's avarice: she has been reverent towards the god and has won his favor. Out of concern for her, the god has started the chain of circumstances that will lead to her happy marriage, one of love and financial security. The girl has been raped at a nighttime festival of Ceres, and, although the god does not admit that as part of his plan, he exploits the crime for her benefit. What he does insist is his doing is: a / Euclio's discovering a treasure buried by his grandfather; b / a rich older man, the uncle of the rapist, asking to marry the pious and seemingly virginal daughter. The girl has not recognized her assailant in the night, but the rapist, Lyconides, does know her identity and will (by the god's plan) marry her. What is lacking in this prologue is any clear indication of the young man's feelings and intentions.

Plautus might have remedied that lack and placed the theme of serious love in a key position in the play, had he desired to, by bringing Lyconides on early to declare his feelings in soliloquy or to indicate them in a scene with one of the principal characters.[11] But Plautus does not wish to distract himself or the audience with what he regards as insignificant and negligible amatory issues. He refuses to equalize the roles of the miser Euclio and the lover Lyconides so as to bring about a reasonable reconciliation of these two antagonistic irresponsibilities. Because the miser plays into his own comic sensibilities, whereas the lover leaves him largely alienated, Plautus lets Euclio upstage Lyconides, and he turns the play into a lively, hilarious comedy about a mad miser.

Lyconides first appears on stage after the mid-point of the plot development (lines 682 ff). In a short scene, which omits all mention of love and feelings (and, I assume, has been radically cut by Plautus), the 'lover' indicates that he has just confessed all to his mother and urged her to intercede with his uncle so that the older man will abandon his marriage plans. At precisely this critical point, the girl goes into labour, and the urgency of Lyconides' request becomes even more obvious. In fewer than twenty lines, he has departed, with no convincing words about the girl; his last five lines refer to his anxiety about his slave, and represent a bridge to the slave's entrance. (The slave has managed to steal Euclio's pot of gold and is carrying it off to his master.)

Lyconides does have one important scene before the manuscript became damaged and so deprived us of the final act. Euclio rushes on stage first, shrieking bloody murder and performing a wonderful routine with the lyric metres and language Plautus has invented for him. When Lyconides hears him howling outside his home, he comes out to see what is the matter, and the key scene (lines 731–807) begins. Up to this point, Euclio has hardly noticed his daughter and, incredibly but most significantly, he does not know that she has been raped or that she has become pregnant or that now she has given birth. For him, the loss of his gold alone counts. In contrast, Lyconides knows nothing about the treasure yet, and he concentrates exclusively on the marriage he desires. Thus, Plautus creates here the finest ancient example of comic cross-purposes and incomprehension (which so fascinated Molière and his admirer, the comic theorist Bergson).[12]

Since Lyconides assumes that Euclio exclaims 'tragically' over
the birth of his grandchild, he quickly confesses to the crime
(*facinus*, line 733). But Euclio focuses on a different 'crime' and
knows nothing of his domestic crisis. So the naïve honesty of
Lyconides serves mainly to expose the weird extremism of a
miser who has entirely ignored his daughter, who has cherished
his pot of gold and tried to conceal it but never noticed the
growing pregnancy of the girl – what we might call a more precious 'treasure.'[13] In the course of his misunderstood confession,
Lyconides declares that he acted under the force of love and
wine (line 745), but Euclio angrily rejects such an excuse.

Having dismissed all discussion of love, Euclio soon breaks
the comic framework of incomprehension by charging Lyconides
with outright theft (line 759). Hereupon, Lyconides asserts himself for the first time in the play, and Euclio yields centre stage
to a man of higher social status and wealth, not to a lover.
Lyconides reveals to the miser two more disasters to climax the
'tragedy' of his lost treasure: namely, the decision of his uncle to
break off marriage arrangements (line 783) and then the details
of the rape nine months earlier (lines 790 ff). Assuming complete
command of the wailing, seemingly broken old man, Lyconides
sends him indoors to talk to his daughter and check on the
details of his story. Although the comic extremism of the miser
has been brought under some control at the end, Plautus has not
balanced it with any convincing emphasis on Lyconides' love.
The pot of gold, not the baby, remains the dominant symbol and
interest of the comedy. As the manuscript fails, we find Lyconides
talking with his slave and learning about the theft. How much
Plautus elaborated this situation is unclear; but the slave tries to
extort his freedom and is in the process of defying Lyconides
when the Latin text ends. Two ancient plot summaries indicate
that eventually Lyconides did resume possession of the pot and
restored it to the overjoyed Euclio, who then happily assented to
the marriage of his daughter.[14] Thus, the comedy ends with the
prospect of happy marriage, but Plautus has given Euclio and his
avarice the dominant role, a role of such lyric and comic energy
that no audience can pay much attention to Lyconides and his
love.

THE KIDNAPPED OR FOUNDLING MAIDEN:
CISTELLARIA AND *CURCULIO*

The other plot type that led to marriage, when the girl has been kidnapped or abandoned and trapped into the world of prostitution (from which Recognition will rescue her during the play), had an advantage the dramatists quickly appreciated: the girl, not confined by family proprieties, but allowed the 'freedom' and the 'free speech' of the courtesan, could both move and speak in public and thus be shown in situations of dramatic action and dialogue to reveal her personality. Moreover, instead of making the father and family the obstacle to love, this type had the monstrous pimp (or bawd) as a much more unappealing killjoy, and the father became the saviour, the loving parent who searched out the daughter and finally rescued and restored her to happiness. Of the four such plays that Plautus has left us, one, the *Rudens*, derives from Diphilos; it dealt with a kidnapped girl. I have already sufficiently described the way Diphilos (and Plautus after him) diminished the love element by keeping the lovers apart and eliminating amatory language and themes. A second, the *Cistellaria*, seems to be a relatively early adaptation from Menander, completed during the Punic War before 200. In its presentation of a very sympathetic foundling, it reveals the anti-romantic Plautus confidently at work, even at that date.[15]

In the opening scene, which gave Menander's play its title (*The Women Breakfasting Together*), Selenium has invited two women to her house, and they chat about life as courtesans before coming to the business at hand, namely, Selenium's misery. Having fallen in love with the first man who hired her services, she has prevailed upon her mother to be allowed to 'live with him' rather than to seek many lovers/customers. For he swears he loves her and will marry her (line 97). This love idyll has lasted a while, but now it has been shattered by the necessity, imposed by his father, that Alcesimarchus, the ardent lover, face reality and marry a very eligible, rich young lady. Selenium is broken-hearted; her companions remark that women are supposed to be heartless (line 66). She laments the bitterness of being in love (line 68), using the same pun as in *Trinummus*,

line 260: *eho an amare occipere amarum est, opsecro*? At the end
of the scene, she goes off, bedraggled and in tears, leaving her
courtesan-friend Gymnasium to face the faithless Alcesimarchus.
And Gymnasium's mother, a hardened bawd, comments: 'Now
that's why I keep pounding it into your ears, never love any
man' (lines 116–17). With only a slight touch of cynical realism,
Plautus has allowed the love of Selenium to be sympathetically
presented, in contrast to the practical courtesans' denial of love
and all feeling.

After the chatty details of a verbose delayed prologue, Plautus
introduces us to the lover, Alcesimarchus, who has hurried back,
he trusts, to Selenium after being kept for six frustratingly te-
dious days in the country at his father's manor. In an entrance
soliloquy, to which Plautus gives his special emphasis by shaping
it as a lyric monody, the young man declares at length how
wretched he feels. Love, he asserts, must have been the inventor
of torture, to judge from his own pains. He exceeds the agonies
of all the men in the world (lines 203 ff). By the overstatement,
where five Latin verbs replace one Greek, where repetition and
alliteration invite us to savour sound more than meaning, and
by the rollicking anapaestic metre, Plautus starts the process of
undermining Alcesimarchus. From the fragmentary state of the
text, it still is possible to infer that, when he found that Selenium
had left him, he went momentarily wild in despair (again, comically exaggerated by Plautus), then charged after her to her
mother's house.

Finding Selenium there, he tries in vain to explain the situation, but neither she nor her mother wants to listen to his 'lies.'
Selenium goes indoors, and Alcesimarchus spends a long time
pleading with her mother, Melaenis, to give him a chance to
prove that he won't marry the girl his father has chosen for him,
that he will remain loyal to Selenium. He launches into a long,
incoherent oath, sworn by a series of gods whose relationships
he gets wrong, forcing Melaenis to interrupt repeatedly to correct him. 'You're bewitching me, and that's why I am making
these mistakes,' he claims (line 517). When she remains unmoved,
his oaths turn into threats, which Plautus also sabotages by
Alcesimarchus' own admission of confusion (*quid dicam nescio,*

line 520) and by the comic intrusions he adds. Here are his sworn threats: 'May all the gods, large, small, and even those of the platter [an irreverent reference to the Lares], deny me the chance while alive to kiss the living Selenium, if I don't butcher you both today, you and your daughter [i.e., Selenium!], then if I don't slaughter you both tomorrow at dawn's first light, and finally, by god, if I don't strike you dead in a third assault – unless you send her back to me. There, I've said what I wanted,' (lines 522–7). Anyone who desires to may try to figure out the logic of all that incoherence, all those repeated murders over a kiss, but it is clear that Plautus aims to make the audience laugh at this lover.

Alcesimarchus stalked away and returned to his empty house, full of anger, self-pity, and despair. Soon after, Plautus turns his attention to the process of getting Selenium recognized. Melaenis, who is not after all the natural mother of Selenium, overhears a conversation which enables her to identify the real mother and realize that she cannot hold on to the girl. 'Now,' she says, 'I must be good against my nature, even though I don't want to be' (lines 626–7), and she decides to restore Selenium to her true parents. Therefore, as she and the girl are walking down the street to the home of those parents, they pass Alcesimarchus' house. Without seeing them at first – though perhaps Plautus used some broad pantomime here to indicate otherwise – the desolate lover prepares to commit suicide there in public. As he loudly invokes Death, 'friend and well-wisher' (line 640), Selenium of course notices him and the sword he histrionically brandishes, in this parody of a tragic suicide (such as that of Ajax). She rushes to stop him; he welcomes her as his salvation; he picks her up and hurries back inside his home and orders his slaves to bar the doors. Thus, on the verge of the recognition, love has impetuously and comically asserted itself. This is the last we see of the two lovers.

The remainder of the play focuses on the melodramatic action which accounts for the Plautine title, *Cistellaria*. In the confusion caused by Alcesimarchus' violent removal of Selenium, the old servant who was carrying the identifying trinkets of the girl in a small casket (*cistella*) dropped it in the street. Plautus pokes fun at the sentimental stages which lead up to the moment of recognition: the old woman is bumbling; the true mother is tearfully anxious; and the servant is roguish, witty, and ribald. But having got us to this big moment of family reunion, Plautus sends everybody indoors, except the caustic slave Lampadio. He is there to greet the last interested character, the long-lost father of Selenium, who wants to know what is happening. Plautus makes sure we take this scene with suitable amusement. In answer to his master's question, the slave pompously declaims: 'I am delighted to inform you that by my efforts you have acquired more children.' 'That does not please me,' the master grumbles. 'I don't like to have more children created for me by another's effort,' (lines 776–8). And with that mild ribaldry Plautus brings down the curtain in another three lines. Menander's delicate love situation has been mocked; the family reunion has been turned into a ridiculous scene over a casket of trinkets; and finally comes a joke about illegitimate children (from the father who was the original sire of Selenium out of wedlock, as they say). And the lovers are ignored by Plautus for the final 125 lines of the comedy, which prefers to plot out of the play their amatory happiness, saccharine and silly to the playwright and his audience, and instead concentrate on foolery. The lover Alcesimarchus has been upstaged by the impudent slave, the pathetic Selenium by the bumbling old Halisca, and Plautus' new comic emphasis has earned Menander's comedy a new title.

In the *Curculio* (*The Weevil*), a play of Plautus' maturity, the love plot and the lover are presented as ridiculous from the opening scene. Again, the girl has been kidnapped as a baby, under the confusion of a storm (lines 644 ff). In this standardized situation, young Phaedromus and his brash slave Palinurus approach the house of a pimp at night. By the dialogue outside, Phaedromus acquaints his cynical slave and us with his silly feelings about love and with the trite details of his infatuation with a young courtesan who, he insists to the incredulous Palinurus, still retains her chastity and has awakened true love in him. Palinurus has no sympathy with such love and mocks all romantic sentiment. Knocking at the door, Phaedromus bribes a bibulous bawd with a jug of wine to let him talk with his beloved Planesium ('The Wandering Girl'). That should have been a brief and incidental bridge scene, but Plautus builds it up into a wonderfully animated comic routine, using his lyric genius to render the rhapsodies of the old soak with her wine and the equally foolish rhapsodies of the lover addressing the closed door. As the one personifies lovingly her wine and the other the bolts of the door, in operatic strains, Plautus and his audience laugh at their folly, the lover's no less than the crone's.

The old bawd leads Planesium anxiously out, trying to avoid any sound for her master the pimp to hear. She puts some water on the door hinges to prevent their creaking, and that provokes the sardonic Palinurus to sneer at her 'medical treatment,': 'She has learned to drink her wine straight, but she gives the doors water to imbibe' (lines 160–1). After that comic crack, Plautus gives Planesium her first lines – florid, alliterative, and artificial. The Latin might be partially captured with the following: 'Where are you who have summoned me to appear at the court sessions of sex?' (*ubi tu's qui me convadatu's Veneriis vadimoniis?* line 162). Phaedromus responds to her in the same high-blown diction, and the only realistic language during this scene of overacted passion comes from Palinurus, who is tired, bored, disgusted, and utterly disenchanted by these lovers. When he tries to break up their embraces and get his master to go home, he earns for himself a beating, which only increases his alienation at this 'crazy' pair. Eventually, Planesium has to go back indoors. The scene ends, then, with a nice contrast between lover and slave. Phaedromus moans emotionally: 'What a beautiful way I have died'; but Palinurus corrects him: 'Not I, who am dead with your beating and sleepiness' (lines 214–15). Down-to-earth reality puts the lover's verbiage in perspective. Although Palinurus may not exactly upstage his master, he prepares the audience to make light of the lover and his amatory plot, so that, when the parasite Curculio appears, he can indeed take over the lead.[16]

Unlike the slave, Curculio acts in a free and enterprising manner and owes no allegiance or advice to Phaedromus: he serves for the food he can get. Thus, he has no interest whatsoever in love for itself, only for what meals it can produce for him. He has a fine impudent entry, in which he assumes the officious airs of a noble, to whom all wayfarers should yield passage (lines 280 ff). And, indeed, all other characters let themselves be up-staged by this energetic and picturesque person. Though he has failed to borrow the money Phaedromus sent him to Caria to get, he has returned confidently with a stolen ring and the means of intrigue, the kind of plot that appeals to Plautus. Donning disguise and employing false documents sealed with this ring's signet, Curculio bilks the loanshark and then the pimp of Planesium. The entire centre of the play features his intrepid activities, and Phaedromus has only a bit part, Planesium none at the same time. Love and lovers have yielded, in Plautus' bi-ased plotting, to intrigue and parasite.

To wind up the plot, it is necessary to make the courtesan an eligible virgin, that is, to have her recognized as a member of a suitable family and become marriageable. All this works itself out with considerable economy. The man whom Curculio de-frauded in Caria of ring and access to the girl, a braggart soldier who typically serves as victim of the lover's henchman, enters furiously and grabs Curculio, who extricates himself neatly when the stolen ring identifies the soldier as brother of Planesium. The recognition, perfunctorily completed in twenty-five lines (635–58), gives the opportunistic and masterful Curculio the cue to stage his final triumph. He urges the soldier to celebrate the recovery of his sister at a banquet today, and Phaedromus to hold an engagement party tomorrow (lines 660–1). And he then presides over the official words of engagement, throwing in his own quixotic 'dowry,' that he will let the groom feed him as long as he lives (line 664)! Curculio has taken over from Palinurus and carried out Plautus' purpose in the plot, to upstage the lover in the most flagrant and impudent manner. The crazy serious-ness of the lover cannot hold its own, in Plautus' theatre, with the witty realism of down-to-earth rogues like Curculio the weevil.

LOVE WHERE MARRIAGE IS IMPOSSIBLE AND IRRELEVANT

In Graeco-Roman society, middle-class and upper-class families could not cope with unions that endangered the family's cohe-sion and economic well-being. Since the family constituted the recognized heart of society, New Comedy tended to contrive plots that enacted the justification and preservation of the family against such centrifugal forces as selfish passion, of young and old alike, and selfish extravagance. An ideal comic myth or scenario developed in which a young man (or, occasionally, a father of the family) fell in love with a courtesan, spent large sums of the family finances on her and even worked to buy her freedom, against the will or without the knowledge of the rest of the family – above all, that of the authority figure (father or wife). The problem of the plot then became to bring this irresponsible love under some control, so that the lover either abandoned it (having come to his senses) or continued it temporarily on a reduced and more practical basis. If he abandoned the courtesan in the play, he probably replaced her with a fiancée;[17] if he was allowed to carry on for a while, it is implicit that eventually he will make the decision to opt for a marriage that benefits family and society. Among the Menandrian comedies that Terence chose for adaptation were several in which the playwright represented both types of irresponsible love, that which carelessly pursued a girl who could eventually be married (though of modest means, pregnant, or incorrectly thought to be a mere prostitute) and that which also carelessly but more dangerously involved itself with a girl who was unquestionably a prostitute with no possibility of change. In the various antitheses that these paired loves permitted, Terence (and Menander before him) threw a carefully angled light on the criteria of legitimate marriage.

Now, imagine a comic artist who perceives in this material, suitably manipulated, a richly comic vein of irreverence and a challenge to traditional romanticism – perhaps, too, to the exclusive dramatic concern with the family lives of the upper classes (of Greece more than of Rome?). He decides to make a mockery of the family and what he can present as its corrupt prejudices, so as to deny its traditional validity in comedy as the criterion and goal of all action. To replace it, he adopts its old enemy, namely, irresponsible love. Not that he views such love with benevolence and generosity, free of the social bias of fourth- and third-century Greek writers. On the contrary, it is the fact that it manifests irresponsibility rather than love that wins his enthusiastic assent, that it opens an avenue to a view of a comic world where the family has little validity, but pleasure earned by witty intrigue of social outcasts constitutes a valid and admirable goal, recognizable by everyone in the audience. Such a comic artist, or even comic genius, I suggest, is Plautus.

A Slave's Intrigue for His Own Prostitute:
Persa

In one comedy, Plautus almost entirely eliminates the criterion of the family, and thus he simplifies the conflict to one between the roguish lover and the infamous pimp. He accomplishes this feat by making the lover a slave and confining his social range to the lowest level: slaves, pimp, parasite, and prostitute. Toxilus proclaims himself a typical lover in a brief opening lyric, and his companion, another slave, remarks with surprise: 'Do slaves now fall in love here?' (*iam servi hic amant*? line 27). Thus, Plautus deliberately calls attention to the way the slave apes the folly of the typical spoiled young Athenian. And Toxilus faces the usual crisis: he needs to buy his girlfriend's freedom from the pimp who owns her. To do this, since of course he lacks money (like the typical *adulescens*), he must resort to intrigue. As a rogue-slave, Toxilus finds intrigue easy enough, but he is a rare beneficiary of intrigue (which most frequently serves the helpless young master).[18]

The plot falls into two phases. First, his slave-friend from another household temporarily 'borrows' money he was supposed to spend on some cattle, and lends it to Toxilus, who then surprises the pimp by paying good cold cash for the girl. Having disarmed the pimp, Toxilus then can develop a plot against him, luring him into purchasing for the same sum a beautiful young girl in exotic dress, who is introduced to him by a pompously masquerading slave as a valuable Arabian captive. In fact, this girl is the freeborn daughter of a parasite, who has willingly cooperated in the plot, in order to earn a good meal. It is of course illegal to purchase a freeborn Athenian, and the purchaser loses both his purchase and the money he paid, once the identity of the girl can be established. Toxilus can then repay his loan, the other slave can buy the oxen, and all can celebrate their victory over the comic villain, the pimp.

The heroic slave Toxilus acts in a context that ignores his normal subservient position: for the duration of the play, his master is away (line 32), and he has the run of the house. His love hurts nobody and no family priorities. It is significant, I think, that his intrigue involves exploiting harmlessly the family situation of the parasite and his daughter. Her appearance as the beauteous 'Arabian' is a mark of her father's enslavement to food, and her typical female cleverness (malitia), a quality of all women in Plautus, slave or free. As a lover, Toxilus is a superb intriguer; but he never becomes the silly, helpless, self-pitying character we usually encounter among the free young lovers. And his energetic invention and participation in the deception of the pimp occupies Plautus' attention and dominates the audience's interest. After the first brief, lyric lover's effusion, the rogue starts to take over. Before the Act I has ended, he has set his companion slave to work and devised a plan that will make use of the parasite, as he confidently announces: 'I have worked out the entire plot, how the pimp with his own money will make her [i.e., his slave] today his freedwoman,' (lines 81–2). There is no further reference to love, amid the spectacularly developing intrigue, and only in the final celebration of victory does the love receive some attention again. Toxilus emerges with a lyric speech of victory, full of pompous Roman language that implies his free heroic status on a par with that of the great Roman generals of the century. No words about love there, as he elaborates the nature of his victory celebration (lines 756 ff). Feeling ignored, the girlfriend, who was ostensibly the reason for all this energetic scheming, asks why she and he are not doing something together (line 763). At that, Toxilus launches himself into an enthusiastic mix of love, drinking, and hilarity, which Plautus enlivens by more lyric. But after thirteen lines of that, the pimp emerges from his house, tragically emoting over his financial loss, and the remainder of the play abandons the love theme in order to exult over the pimp's misery. That comic situation merits almost one hundred lines of Plautine excitement, and the final word of the slave is from the triumphant intriguer,

not the gratified lover: *leno perit* (line 857) – 'The pimp is dead!'
In a significant way, then, Toxilus the lover has been upstaged
by Toxilus the rogue.

Gratifying Foolish Young Love:
Pseudolus

The initial situation of *Curculio* and *Persa*, the desperate desire
of the impecunious lover to buy free the beloved courtesan owned
by the pimp, recurs frequently in the plays of Plautus where
marriage is irrelevant. Buying free a woman whom one can never
marry constitutes the height of romantic folly. Yet in Plautine
comedy after comedy, the woman does get her freedom at great
expense. However, that freedom proves to be less a tribute to the
beauty and desirability of the woman than a means to assert
Plautus' theme – that sensual pleasure achieved by unscrupu-
lous roguery merits our applause, at least on the stage. In some
plays, like *Mercator* and *Mostellaria*, the young lover has bought
the beloved free before the dramatized action starts, and that
unwise purchase provides an initial complication. In others,
finding the money to free the girl provides an opening for the
intrepidity of the slave or parasite. I shall consider *Pseudolus* in
this light.

Pseudolus has no more respect for the romantic love of his
young master, Calidorus, than does Palinurus for that of
Phaedromus in *Curculio*. When Calidorus gets hysterical with
helplessness and tries to borrow a drachma from Pseudolus so as
to buy a rope and hang himself, the slave delights us by his
practical question: 'Who will pay me back the drachma if I give
it to you? Do you intend to hang yourself deliberately so as to
cheat me?' (lines 91–3). Nevertheless, realizing how useless
Calidorus is, Pseudolus promises to get him the needed money
somewhere, somehow. And with the brashness born of years of
successful roguery, he publicly proclaims to all his friends and
acquaintances to beware today, not to trust him in any way, or
else they will be bilked (lines 124 ff).

Plautus makes clear his concentration on Pseudolus, the ironic
facilitator of love, but even more the master-trickster (as his

name implies), by giving no speaking part to Phoenicium, the prostitute so passionately desired by the young fool. After Calidorus fails to make any impression on the arch-villain Ballio the pimp, Pseudolus sends him off to find a clever man who will be able to get things done (line 393). In other words, Calidorus must locate a man who can do for him what he, in his ineptitude, cannot do for himself. Left to his own resourceful devices, Pseudolus improvises in several encounters, and actually has a workable plan by the time Calidorus returns with a friend who will provide the trusted helper (line 693). Calidorus has subordinated himself to Pseudolus, and at the end of this scene (line 758) he disappears from the comedy. Although the play is hardly half-finished, Plautus insists on so upstaging the lover as to remove him from the stage, so that the intrigue can have his and the audience's undivided attention.

When Calidorus vanishes from the play, Plautus makes it clear that the lines of thematic opposition do not focus on the family and pit father against son. Rather, they focus on money, on the stern father who wants to hold on to his wealth and his dubious ally, the pimp, who wants to make as much money from his exploited prostitutes as possible. This pair hopes to keep Pseudolus the trickster in check. As Pseudolus celebrates his triumph in Act V, he drunkenly describes the scene of sexual revelry in which Calidorus has participated, and Pseudolus, too. The slave has earned his pleasures, and it is appropriate that he be the one to report them. But his supreme pleasure involves his 'victory' over his cheerless and angry old master, Simo: to that Plautus devotes the finale of the play. Thus, not only does the young lover yield the stage to the slave, but the old master has to act out Pseudolus' superiority.[19]

Guilty Elderly Love Balked:
Asinaria

The old man in love (*senex amator*) was a ridiculous figure, pursuing an activity which, by comic definition, was reserved for young men. To ensure our bias, the dramatist regularly insisted that this untimely lover was already married and thus had primary responsibility to his wife and household. We have already seen how Demipho in the *Mercator* unwittingly competed with his own son over a courtesan and finally was disgraced and shamed, though it was agreed that his wife would not know anything. In the early *Asinaria*, the father, Demaenetus, plays the role of a rather black-hearted rogue who cheats his wife out of money to buy a prostitute free for his son, then turns around and tries to exploit the situation so as to enjoy the girl before his son can. Theoretically, Plautus could have emphasized romantic love quite easily in such a situation, by contrasting the real affection of the son with the sleazy lust of the father. But the playwright shows his concern to ridicule both lovers and subject them and their warped passion to humiliation.

The son, Argyrippus, loves the courtesan Philaenium, but has no money to keep up the relation; and her greedy mother insists on a sizeable sum to guarantee Philaenium's exclusive services for a year. Although Philaenium seems to be an unwilling victim of her mother and, despite her cruel situation, eager to respond to Argyrippus' love, Plautus interrupts their single scene of romance (lines 590 ff) with a raucous series of pranks by a pair of slaves, who humiliate both lovers and show how much they will compromise their love for money. Argyrippus stands helplessly aside while Philaenium all but makes love to the slaves, as the price of the stolen money, then allows the slaves to ride him as a donkey, acting out the reversed roles in the household. Thus, young love is first upstaged, in preparation for the upstaging of older love and for the final feeling in the audience that love in general has yielded to something realer and better: roguish humour and wit.

When Demaenetus introduces himself and his purposes, he says nothing about his pursuit of prostitutes in his old age. Instead, he declares himself to be an unusual father, in that he expresses full support for his son's affair with Philaenium, the prostitute in the house next door (line 53). He sides with the son against his wife, who has full control of the money in the household – presumably, it all comes from her family – and keeps a tight rein on the son's sexual extravagances. (It also emerges later, but not here, that she has been cramping the style of

Demaenetus as a would-be old lover.) With no sense of financial responsibility, then, well practised in cheating his wife to finance his own illicit pleasures, the father happily encourages the boy's loyal slaves to engage in any malpractice, with his full cooperation, to swindle the wife of the necessary money for Philaenium. 'I want to be loved by my family,' he grandly claims (line 67); but, since he doesn't include his hated wife, he really means: 'I want my son to love me, his father' (line 77). At first sight, then, if we ignore the culpable attitude towards the rich wife, it might seem that Demaenetus is one of those endearing contrasts to the stern and angry father: he seems like the kindly, supportive, and tolerant father (*lepidus pater, senex*). And, indeed, it is he in person, we are told, who acted decisively to ensure that the slaves' trickery actually succeeded. So the slaves admit as they praise his congenial nature (line 580).

In fact, Demaenetus is a hypocritical old reprobate, but Plautus has minimized the full facts about him so as to spring them on us suddenly at the end of the comedy. Family love means little to this father, much less than the lust he pursues at every opportunity, and notably here, in the case of Philaenium, whom he boldly tries to exploit at this opportunity. After Argyrippus has been forced to submit to humiliation from the slaves, he learns that he has more humiliation to accept. His good old dad has made the money available, the slaves are to report, on condition that Argyrippus allow his father to enjoy a dinner and night of sex with Philaenium (lines 735–6). Argyrippus' craven character cooperates, as Demaenetus knew he would, with his own baseness: he agrees to his father's terms. The servants, having had their fun and delivered their heartless but grotesquely amusing message, prepare to leave, and the young lover bids them farewell (*valete*). They reply, also using the plural: 'And you, too, love well' (*et vos amate*, line 745). That plural may apply only to Argyrippus and Philaenium, who stand there rather forlornly on stage: or it may include also Demaenetus (soon to appear). At any rate, the irony of the final remark is unmistakable and would no doubt have been emphasized by the roguish speaker.[20]

The stage is set here for the reappearance of the father, now revealed as hypocritical old lover (*senex amator*) rather than a kindly and indulgent paternal figure. But, before his entrance, Plautus introduces us to the angry young man who will bring about his punishment. Of about the same age as Argyrippus, but with the money to satisfy his own passions, this character shows the spunk absent in the son. He intends to inform Demaenetus' wife, Artemona, and thus humble the old lover for his robberies. In the finale, then, as Demaenetus starts to enjoy his pleasure in front of the pained but compliant Argyrippus, Artemona secretly enters, to watch and overhear with indignation her husband's outrages. He promises to steal a robe from Artemona for Philaenium; he kisses her lustily and comments on the sweet breath she has, which is so wonderful after his wife's halitosis; he wishes that the wife may be destroyed 'with interest,' so that he won't be interrupted while kissing; and finally, he invokes Venus to grant to him Philaenium and to his wife, death. At that, Artemona no longer restrains herself, but bursts into the corrupt celebration and commands Demaenetus: 'Get up, lover, and go home!' (surge, amator, i domum, line 921). He slinks off, totally humbled and terrified, awaiting the judgment that will be meted out to him at home (line 937). Enjoying their moment, Argyrippus and Philaenium taunt him and his promises. Not much can be said for romantic love after this comedy; and, indeed, the final comments of the assembled troupe to the audience urge the amoral moral, that anyone, if he had the chance, would act like Demaenetus and pursue his own satisfactions (lines 944–5). Plautus does not use untimely old love as a way of validating young love, but rather as a way of utterly discrediting romantic love: all love, young and old, is a prime target for his comedy.

The Courtesan Mocks the Lover:
Truculentus

In the comedies we have been using as examples in this section, the impecunious young man – helpless, ridiculous, and far less interesting to Plautus than the rogues and scamps that both help and interfere with the course of his love – eventually gets to take his courtesan-friend to bed, for a while. The lover and his love have proved to be of minimal comic sympathy and regularly replaceable with characters and qualities that make a mockery of romance and rather validate an energetic, resourceful engagement with a more ordinary reality that thumbs its nose at feckless feelings. The audience's attitude can also be affected by the manner in which the courtesan behaves. We have seen Philaenium of the *Asinaria* play the naïve affectionate girl, at the start of the play, until she gets caught up in the tricks of the libidinous slaves and old father. Her natural innocence helps to put in the desired satirical perspective the hypocritical lust of the males, father and son. In the *Pseudolus*, Phoenicium never says a word and appears only once, to be led silently weeping and unknowing from the house of the pimp Ballio to reunion with Calidorus. Both she and her lover are suppressed, upstaged by the trickster slave. In the *Bacchides*, the courtesan sisters are delightfully seductive, but definitely not ruled by their affections. They seduce Pistoclerus at the opening, to escape an unwelcome debt to a soldier; throughout the play their seductiveness determines the efforts of Mnesilochus and his slave Chrysalus; and in the finale they complete their victorious campaign by seducing the two fathers. Therefore, although we can say that the young lovers, after being upstaged, have gotten their satisfaction at the end, Plautus' emphasis rests on the triumphant courtesans, who celebrate not love but their successful manipulation of men in the interests of security. In the *Truculentus*, which is a work of Plautus' old age, the satisfaction of young lovers and the sensual pleasures of all disappear from the comic plot: with a strong satiric tone, the comedy focuses on the materialistic success of the courtesan, gained at the expense of stupid would-be lovers. The lover has been conclusively upstaged, and deservedly so, by the totally self-serving Phronesium, the woman of ruthless intelligence. An independent operator, like the Bacchides, she owes nothing to any pimp, but works exclusively for her own advantage.

There are three lovers, and none of them gets to take Phronesium to bed, but each pays extravagantly for the vain hope that he will get his money's worth. The yokel Strabax comes to Athens from the country, shaggy, unkempt, and boorish, the last person in the world that anyone could love. But he serves Phronesium's purposes well: he is easily controlled by her, and his very unlikely nature can whet the jealousy of other potential lovers. When he appears from the farm, naïvely carrying money which belongs to his father (lines 653–5), the eyes of Phronesium's smart female slave fall on the money, and she invites Strabax indoors. An hour or so later, he emerges and complains that he is exhausted from having waited for his 'friend' inside, lying in the bed (lines 915–16). But that arrival plays into the hands of Phronesium, who is talking to the soldier Stratophanes and wheedling him out of money by lies about a supposed child of his that she has borne while he was absent on campaign. Stratophanes gets angrily jealous and plunges into a 'war' of rival gifts, which the courtesan, of course, brilliantly directs. Although the two go together into the courtesan's house then, promising themselves sexual satisfaction, we are not convinced, especially since Phronesium stays behind to exult before the audience on the success of her 'hunt' for silly bird-victims (lines 964–5).

The yokel and the soldier are two typical losers in the love plots of New Comedy, and we are not surprised to see them cancel each other out, even if Phronesium's materialistic exploitation seems unusually overstressed. But the third lover comes from the most respectable level of Athenian society. He has had a long, expensive relationship with the courtesan in the past, but been forced out when Phronesium got her hooks into the more extravagant Stratophanes. Just back from a minor diplomatic trip, he starts the play off with a soliloquy on the crippling cost of courtesan-love and the ruinous greed of pimps and prostitutes. On his return, he has incredulously heard that Phronesium has had a baby (lines 85–6); it does not seem likely to him that so clever a courtesan would ever permit herself to get pregnant and ruin her business. So it must be a trick to control the soldier, he thinks. And he is jealous and eager to become her lover again. Promising to bankrupt his estates, he gets himself admitted to the house (lines 175 ff). But he, too, is disappointed after a long wait: Phronesium is taking an interminable bath (lines 320 ff). He does eventually get to talk with her, and her friendliness (activated by her not too subtle greed) sends him off cheerily to pawn his property and buy her a lavish gift (lines 425–6).

Evidently, Diniarchus, the affluent young diplomat, is as much a fool for love as the rustic and the soldier. However, he emerges soon as more contemptible than laughable, a young man whose status has encouraged him into irresponsible and reprehensible self-indulgence. The baby, which Phronesium has confessed to him is not hers, much to his delight, and which he then laughs to see being used against the gullible soldier, turns out to be his, Diniarchus'. He had had an illegitimate affair with a respectable Athenian girl; she became pregnant and gave birth during his absence, and she abandoned or exposed the baby to avoid embarrassment. Thus, the baby proves to embarrass Diniarchus more than anybody, and, just after he has lavished presents on Phronesium, it obliges him to confess his paternity and accept marriage to the girl. Then, to emphasize how low Diniarchus has sunk, Plautus shows this new 'father' happily conspiring with Phronesium to lend her his baby so that she can complete her scam of the foolish soldier (and later, Diniarchus hopes, reward Diniarchus with a night or two of 'love').

Male love, accordingly, is totally discredited in the characterization of these two fools and of the scoundrel Diniarchus. Now, consider the object of their love in Plautus' satiric representation. Phronesium, whose name has nothing to do with love or physical attraction, the usual source of courtesan's names in Plautus, is the thinker or calculator. She herself never feels love – never expresses genuine affection for anyone, male or female – but easily manipulates the language of love in order to gain material profit. The fact that she has pretended to have given birth to a son, which we know from the prologue (line 18), symbolizes clearly her calculating exploitation of words, acts, and feelings of love. Indirectly introduced by the words of Diniarchus about his subjection to her and by the impudent remarks of her maid Astaphium (= Raisin), who has a lyric solo about the ruthless 'philosophy' of prostitutes (lines 209 ff), Phronesium finally makes her first entrance at line 352. She immediately starts her act, using calculated amatory language to enthral the easily duped Diniarchus. He has waited endlessly, remember, for her to finish her so-called bath, and he feels grouchy. 'Do you think my doorway will bite you, tell me, that you are afraid to enter, my sweetheart?' (lines 352–3). 'Why are you so grumpy on your return from Lemnos as not to give your girlfriend a kiss?' (lines 355–6). By the end of the scene, sullen Diniarchus has become putty in her artful hands. He calls her 'Sweetheart' at the very moment he happily succumbs to her wiles and declares it a 'profit' to himself when she asks him for a gift (*lucrum hercle videor facere mihi, voluptas mea, ubi quippiam me poscis*, lines 426–7). And he gullibly misconstrues, as she intended, her confession about the fake baby as utter proof of her deepest, most reliable love (lines 434 ff).[21]

The women of this comedy, Phronesium the heroine and her bawd-maid Astaphium, encourage the three foolish male lovers in their folly and deliberately exploit them and the trappings of love for personal material profit. Their real thinking assumes a hostile world and militant behaviour against lovers. 'A lover is like an enemy city,' says Astaphium. 'As soon as he can be taken, he is great for his girlfriend' (lines 170–1). 'A proper bawd should have good teeth,' reflects Phronesium, 'so that she can laugh and smoothly speak to every visitor, plotting evil in her heart, but speaking good with her tongue' (lines 224–7). 'The good lover,' she adds, 'is the man who abandons all his possessions and destroys his estate.' The women measure and value men for their money: the men throw away money in pursuit of their false conception of love, which they ludicrously identify with these mercenary women. It is not unusual or disturbing that the men get what they clearly deserve: no love and heavy losses. What is unusual is the total success of the unromantic and antihedonistic courtesans. There is no celebration at the end of this comedy, because, although Phronesium has scored a complete victory and, as she exults, had a wonderful 'hunt' (line 964), her grasping, insensitive nature does not open up to sensual indulgence and careless spending of any kind. Plautus has exposed the ways of love in the most uncompromising satire, making love, not the 'breath of life' in the comedy, but the touch of death. The courtesan sucks the wealth of the stupid lover (like Diniarchus) and considers him 'dead' when he has no more to give (lines 164–5). Her house resembles Acheron (the home of

Death): once it receives anything, it refuses to disgorge it again
to Life (lines 749–50).

CHAPTER FOUR

Heroic Badness *(malitia)*: Plautus' Characters and Themes

If you can remember your own childhood, or if you have watched and listened to children as they were playing, you perhaps have observed how very important to them are those simple moral terms 'bad' and 'good.' Not, I hasten to say, that children are entirely innocent, naïve, and narrowly puritanical about their use of such terms. Along with the powerful word 'No!,' they have been hearing parents, grandparents, and siblings smiling-and-cooing at them 'Good' and growling, shrieking, and roaring at them 'Bad,' often with gestures and various movements, including pats, spanks, and blows, that ought to have made the meaning of 'bad' and 'good' amply clear – that ought to have aligned them solidly and safely on the side of Good against Bad. Why is it, then, that the little imps get the message twisted and somehow, at an early age, show that they have a sneaking admiration of Bad, that they even want to play at being bad? Let us dismiss with contempt the child who has, alas, gotten the official message too well and says to his or her unruly playmate: 'You're bad; what you're doing is naughty; I'm going to tell Daddy or Mama, and you're going to get it.' There's a future supporter of Law and Order with the character of a skunk. No, the children I refer you to are those we overhear in a conversation like this: A (with a note of admiration): 'Mother said that was naughty. How can you hope to get away with it?' B (with bravado): 'I dunno, but it's fun being naughty.' These are children whom I think we all know (recalling our own behaviour in childhood) and probably rather like, for their humanity if not for their obedience. In this chapter I shall be considering how Plautus explored this fundamental 'immoral' tendency in all of us, children and adults, and gave it comic form as Heroic Badness, which is one of the great achievements of Roman and comic literature.

As parents know, the tendency in children to go astray over the words 'No!' and 'Bad!' starts somewhat before they reach the age of two. When my son approached that age, with his boyish energy and gusto he revealed just how stubbornly the human soul cherishes the simple idea of Bad. It did not matter to him whether what we called Bad was Dangerous, Hot, Cruel, Messy, Dirty, Tiresome, or What-have-you: if we said it was bad, then it had to have something interesting, pleasurable, and hence 'good,' about it. It had to be tried. And the threat and experience of spanking only increased the challenge. I think that, if my son had had a younger brother, the irrepressible way he went about playing with matches, climbing and falling from trees, opening and crawling out windows, etc., would have made him a 'hero' to his younger sibling at the same time that he was driving his parents and sisters to distraction. I am no psychologist and do not intend to explore the psychological motivations for this Original Sin in all human beings, but I am interested in the way, as Milton's Lucifer willed it, evil becomes good in comedy as well as in tragedy and epic, but with a very different plot and audience reception, above all, in Plautus. Among some teenagers today, one can hear exactly the words and note that the Roman poet long ago struck: admiration for what is called Badness. I wish to go back to Plautine Rome to see how he elicited that admiration in his comedies.

The particular kind of badness which I call 'heroic' turns up in the favourite form of Plautine comedy, that of intrigue, where a character or characters use various means of deception to swindle money or the possession of a slave-prostitute from the rightful owners. The deceivers, like the slave Chrysalus and the Bacchis-sisters of the play I reviewed in chapter 1, come from the lower ranks of the social order and can be declared 'bad' in social terms by those above them, their victims. But what is more important, for Plautus' presentation, is that social inferiority goes hand-in-hand with (and, to some extent, stimulates) a striking indifference to strict ethical tenets; an adaptability to conditions; an energetic curiosity; basic cunning and enjoyment of deception; a combative, anarchic attitude towards life; and total indifference to such ordinary things as property rights, duty, responsibility, truth, or authority – in other words, social badness merely covers a much more interesting and universal ethical quality, which might be labelled 'Badness' and praised or punished in the course of a comedy, but is, in fact, a compound of bad and good, as the most attractive comic qualities usually prove to be. It is an obvious fact that Plautus aligns his audiences on the side of the deceivers, for all their badness, against the people who usually control Law and Order, fathers, mothers, rich men, and property-owners (nicely symbolized by the frequent victim, the pimp, the slave-owner of certain desirable prostitutes).

If Plautus' main concern were the sociopolitical hostility between the deprived and the rich, between slaves and slave-owners, as some modern theorists have argued, who have read into Plautus contemporary political antagonisms, then the comic nature of Badness would have no function and not appear.[1] As it is, however, what dominates audience interest and made the plays of Plautus successful at all levels of society – and still does – is the way Badness represents the personal response of every member of the audience, the will to explore, experience, and enjoy what our parents and all authority figures brand as Bad, that is, what often looks to us as perhaps dangerous, but mighty Good. It follows that, if a bad goal appeals to our imaginations as somehow good, then the so-called bad man or woman who pursues and achieves it, even if briefly, appears not only good but heroic, a kind of paradigm of our pipedreams.

The basic scheme from which the plot started was the need of a young man for money to pursue a love affair, in Plautus regularly an affair that has to be 'illicit' and temporary and stupidly wasteful ('bad' from the viewpoint of parents and greybeards), but understandably appealing precisely because it is a reckless move towards sensual pleasure. Since the young man lacks worldly experience and street skills, he desperately turns to the domestic slave, who is usually five or ten years older than he, and centuries older in practical experience. This slave has defied his owner, the boy's father, before and is regarded as a typical 'bad slave,' often declared to be 'worse than any other slave' or simply 'the worst slave in existence' (*servus pessimus*).[2] To the young master, however, many aspects of this badness look hopeful and useful, and he implores and finally persuades this 'bad slave' to do what has become for the love-addled young man a definite good. In their conversation, Plautus rather typically has master and slave articulate this inversion not only of good and bad, but also of their own social roles.

The boy ends up by hailing the slave as his 'patron' as he himself assumes the subordinate role of needy 'client.'[3] Then, the slave assumes masterful airs: he talks about his civil and military authority (Latin *imperium*), and he calls his companions into a senatorial session, to take counsel and plan their strategy. In other words, this base slave (whom we can imagine as originally foreign, non-italian, reduced to slavery as a result of military defeat) arrogates to himself the status of the highest political position in Rome, the consul, and treats himself as an official in wartime, about to lead his troops forth on a critical campaign on behalf of his country.[4] The goals of this expedition, however, fall comically short of the level of nobility. To be consonant, after all, with the purposes of the deception, this commander must come away with a considerable amount of money in the form of 'booty' or 'plunder' (Latin *praeda*). So there is no question about saving the country or avenging some defeat or some other misdeed of the enemy: this special army seeks booty.[5] In due course, the deception achieves its end: the enemy-father or pimp is swindled out of the necessary money, which the slave-general triumphantly carries off as plunder to his anxiously waiting young master. Then, it remains to be seen whether reality catches up with this fantastic slave, whether he plunges back down from his improbably and tenuously won Good to his proper role as 'bad slave,' at the mercy of his humiliated and irate master.

In the great comedies of Plautus' maturity, the playwright managed to twist the plot so that, with full audience approval, reality was pleasantly deflected or excluded. I shall come back to that, but, for the present, it suffices to sketch out the Plautine pattern. To put it briefly, as soon as the tricky bad slave takes on the Mission Impossible of helping out his young master in a quest for money for love, he becomes 'good,' surrounded with symbols of freedom and Roman dignity and authority, admired by his friends and feared by his intended victims for the very same qualities – trickiness, deceptivity, plausibility, adaptability, and restless energy. His 'goodness' is merely 'badness' seen from a new viewpoint. Or, in the Latin terms Plautus employs to epitomize his comic ethical paradox, the clever intriguing slave, whose character can be summarized by the word *malitia* (badness), aims at a goal which in conventional Roman terms is the proud one of military conquest of a despised enemy, the highest achievement of manliness (*virtus*). Since *virtus* extends its meaning in Latin then to cover what we call 'virtue' and what the Romans meant by 'goodness,' the Plautine representation of intrigue is one of badness becoming, with our enthusiastic approval, goodness.[6]

The Plautine intriguer, as is obvious, falls into the class of wonderful comic characters that we recognize as rogues. There seem to be no rogues in Menander; I am not sure that there were any in either of the other masters of Greek New Comedy, Philemon or Diphilos.[7] It looks, at any rate, as though this special rogue, who makes a virtue of his badness (*malitia*), is Plautus' contribution not only to New Comedy in Rome, but to the comic genre. Granted that Aristophanes had worked out the designs of a delightful rogue in the late fifth century, but that was an Athenian rogue, a free man or woman with a different manner of operation and a quite different ethical stance.[8] So, even if Plautus did have some knowledge of Aristophanes – which remains doubtful to many scholars – his Roman rogue emerges as a strikingly new creation. It is the express emphasis on the dialogue between good and bad within the rogue, the focus on his Roman *virtus*, his 'heroic' military enterprise and success, that defines the comic invention of Plautus.

I think that I can make the nature of Plautus' heroic rogue somewhat clearer by turning to another marvellous rogue in his moment of roguish heroism. I refer to Shakespeare's Falstaff and his role during the Battle of Shrewsbury, in Act V of *Henry the Fourth, Part I.* Just before the battle starts, Shakespeare lets us assess the combatants in their respective camps. In Scene 1, we survey the King and his supporters, his princely sons Hal and John, and Falstaff. One by one, they leave the stage, solemnly prepared to do their best to fight bravely, and Hal, before departing, recommends to Falstaff, the last man, to say his prayers and farewell, to face the fact that he owes God a death. It is his simple heroic responsibility to be a man.

This, however, is no metaphorical battle of swindling, and Falstaff feels notably uncomfortable and out of his natural element. Alone, then, he delivers his famous soliloquy, a superb comic speech in the best Shakespearean vein: "'Tis not due yet [i.e., the death mentioned by Prince Hal]: I would be loath to pay him [i.e., God] before his day. What need I be so forward with him that calls not on me? Well, 'tis no matter; honour pricks me on. Yea, but how if honour pricks me off when I come on? How then? Can honour set to a leg? No. Or an arm? No. Or take away the grief of a wound? No. Honour hath no skill in surgery then? No. What is honour? A word. What is that word, honour? Air. A trim reckoning! Who hath it? He that died o' Wednesday. Doth he feel it? No. Doth he hear it? No. Is it insensible, then? Yea, to the dead. But will it not live with the living? No. Why? Detraction will not suffer it. Therefore I'll none of it: honour is a mere scutcheon. And so ends my catechism.'[9]

There is much common as well as comic sense in what Falstaff has said here. This battle is not simply a question of honour; the political values being contested are ambiguous; and the most obvious embodiment of honour, Hotspur, is ridiculed as a fool by his own closest, so-called friends. So when Falstaff rejects honour and advocates the traditional creed of the practical rogue – 'he who fights and runs away, lives to fight another day' – the audience sympathizes.[10] But when the battle ensues, and other men fight, and some die for their partly honourable goals – including loyal Blount on behalf of the king and the enthusiast Hotspur for his personal glory – when Hal risks his life to defend his father, then Falstaff's words and roguish behaviour cannot withstand inspection, cannot continue to command approval. During the battle, although he finally engages in combat with Douglas, he suddenly falls down motionless and pretends to be dead, thus saving his life. Almost at the same moment, Hotspur, who has challenged Hal for supreme honour, falls to the ground mortally wounded and really dies.

The pejorative effect on our impression of Falstaff is obvious. But Shakespeare has worse to show about this rogue. As soon as Hal goes off to continue fighting, Falstaff gets up, easily and confidently, smoothly mouths his 'heroic' creed, that the better part of valour is discretion,[11] and then gets his supreme idea of roguish heroism: he stabs the corpse of Hotspur with his sword and starts to lug the body off, to claim it as *his* honour that the enemy is dead, to claim a reward for *his* 'valour.' It is a fraud that has to strike us as grotesquely ignoble and unfunny, especially since Prince Hal, who knows the truth, makes no effort to reclaim his own credit as hero; he shows his undoubted and well-earned moral superiority by dismissing the whole situation as the act of 'the strangest fellow' and allowing Falstaff to pose as noble and worthy of reward. We may have some questions about honour still, but Shakespeare leaves no doubt about what manliness has required here.[12]

Whereas Shakespeare drags the reluctant rogue on to the real battlefield and, by juxtaposing him with genuine warriors who accept war's creed, shows him up as a coward and rat, Plautus lets his rogue-plotter celebrate his success, the result of his witty deception over others' folly and avarice, and we recognize him as the 'best' person in the play. All the others, those who have been his victims and those who have shared in his intrigue, have been inferior to him. So the metaphorical language which has been building up during the comedy – that the master-plotter is like a consul at war, commander of an army on campaign against a powerful and rich enemy – properly soars to a climax at the moment of success, in a triumphant speech, typically in flamboyant lyric metre (clear proof that it is a Plautine production, not just a translation of the Greek).

The greatest of these triumphant effusions is spoken by the slave Chrysalus in *The Bacchis-Sisters*. It occupies more than fifty lines (925–78) and is a rollicking performance, an actor's dream and the audience's delight. Chrysalus is so full of himself that he compares himself favourably with the best heroes of the

Trojan War, not only with Agamemnon who commanded the expedition, but also with his brother Menelaus (husband of Helen) and with Ulysses who, known by Chrysalus to have been 'bold and bad' (*audacem et malum*, line 949), provides the perfect heroic paradigm for his claim to heroism. But Chrysalus' monody is but the extreme example of a typical Plautine context. Accordingly, a short section of an anapaestic triumph-song from one of the less-well-known comedies, *The Persian*, will illustrate the general type: 'The enemy are beaten, the citizens are safe, the situation's calm, total peace is achieved, / The war's at an end, the campaign was well waged, without loss to the troops, without hurt to the camp. / Lord Jupiter, since it was by your kind help and the other gods mighty in heaven, / I feel and give thanks to you all in this hymn, that I fitly took vengeance this day on my foe. / For that reason now, to all who shared in the fight, I'll give shares of the plunder, division of the spoil' (*hostibus victis, civibu' salvis, re placida, pacibus perfectis, / bello exstincto, re bene gesta, integro exercito et praesidiis, / quom bene nos, Iuppiter, iuvisti, dique alii omnes caelipotentes, / eas vobis gratis habeo atque ago, quia probe sum ultus meum inimicum. / nunc ob eam rem inter participes dividam praedam et participabo* [*Persa*, lines 753–7]).[13]

The speaker is the slave Toxilus who has engineered a scam against a pimp he hates, in order to cheat him out of a large sum of money, the purchase price of a prostitute. The scam has been a total success, and in these lines Toxilus, acting like a victorious Roman commander, proclaims verbosely his achievements – total, bloodless victory no less – gives thanks to the gods, and then proceeds to the final phase of a triumph – the sharing of the booty with the soldiers and the large-scale public celebration, with much food, wine, and love, of the war's happy conclusion.

This victory of Toxilus and the wild celebration that follows are wonderful comic action for Plautus' audience, and they enjoy without reserve the wild performance of this 'heroic' slave. That a slave should be the cleverest person in the comedy, that he should be able to make comic sense by posing as the supreme commander of the free Roman population, that he could wage a heroic campaign against a pimp and convincingly heroize what is nothing but fraud, is entirely acceptable to the audience of free Romans as a fantasy in which they can imaginatively participate: the ability of the little man to succeed by native wit. Let Dordalus the pimp enter raging against Toxilus as the worst of scoundrels (*pessimus corruptor*, line 779): we watch the slave and his fellow conspirators enjoy their physical well-being and even go on to tease unmercifully the helpless, furious Dordalus. The theme of war, triumph, and the honour of military success does not function as a corrective, to expose the base roguery of this slave, but rather to ratify his grandeur, to guarantee that we fall in with his wild fantasy. The lowest and 'worst' member of the population has earned the right, by his sheer energetic use of street wisdom, to be regarded as the best of all: a true Roman hero. Thus, Plautus' comic part for Toxilus differs radically from that designed for Falstaff. Falstaff had to be isolated, exposed as a basically bad man, and then dismissed from the final scene of victory; but Toxilus has, indeed, been the cause of this metaphorical 'victory,' and so becomes the very centre of triumphant celebration.[14]

This conception of 'heroic badness,' we may be pretty certain, did not come to Plautus from his Greek originals, nor was it fully developed in Plautus' imagination at the time he began his career as comic playwright – which, in turn, means that it did not come from his Roman predecessors, such as Naevius and Livius Andronicus, nor directly from some parallel native Italian form of farce. It is worth while, I believe, sketching out a line of development for this key theme, and I shall suggest that *The Bacchis-Sisters*, with which we are quite familiar by now, occupies a pivotal position in my proposed scheme.

One intrigue play has survived from Greek New Comedy in sufficient fullness (namely, in three acts) so that we know how the deceiver operated, and we can observe that, in accordance with expectations, he is neither bad nor a heroic rogue. Menander's comedy *The Shield*, which has been known for less than twenty years, since its lucky recovery from Egypt, depicts the efforts of an entire family to thwart the greedy scheme of a selfish uncle to claim money left by his supposedly dead nephew, a very successful mercenary soldier, and (since that is the legal condition on which he can get the money) to claim also the hand of his young niece. The uncle is the first surviving example of a Menandrian villain, and his villainy, whose symptoms are avarice and violation of the natural order of love, consists essentially in disruption of the integrity and good order of the family. The deceiver proves to be a slave, who indeed devises a very clever scheme and enjoys himself immensely in the process, but he functions as a loyal slave, devoted to his dead master and the welfare of the family. His deception is not anarchic at all, not designed to encourage the wasteful, unwise passion of an irresponsible young master, but it promotes the best interests of the household and frustrates the anarchic intentions of the bad uncle.[15] It is only appropriate, then, that a good older member of the family (in fact, another uncle, the antitype of the villain) participates in the deception. We don't have the final two acts of the comedy and cannot assert exactly how the slave was handled at the end, but it seems pretty clear to me that he would not have stood out as a figure of 'grandiose badness,' or even as a very important character, once he had served his function in the intrigue. For the intrigue was only one thread in a complicated romantic plot which eventually brought the supposedly dead nephew back to Athens and then, we assume, climaxed in a betrothal of two young couples, thus ensuring the future happiness of the family. In those developments, the slave would play no significant part; it appears that he had the pleasure of welcoming his beloved master home in Act IV, but thereafter yielded to other family members.[16]

If we had more of *The Double-Deceiver*, the Menandrian comedy Plautus adapted for his *Bacchis-Sisters*, we might have a more useful example of the limits imposed by Greek comedy on the rogue. The prototype of the flamboyant Chrysalus, who runs verbal riot in the centre of Plautus' comedy and plays repeatedly on the various possibilities of his name, had the ordinary name Syros in Menander; that is, he came originally from Syria. We know that he told a story to the father that resembled the tale Chrysalus spins for Nicobulus on his arrival in port. But no evidence survives to prove how the 'second deception' went, or what then happened for an ending. I have conjectured in chapter

1 that Plautus has suppressed Menander's final act and replaced it with his own creation, that emphasizes the anarchic, irresponsible, anti-family qualities which I consider patently non-Menandrian. Menander, I believe, would have made a more sympathetic and valid authority figure in his father, who was able at the end, with the Greek audience's full assent, to reassert his authority over the anarchic son and his slave and to reunite the family. Syros would have had no magnificent speech of triumph – not in lyrics, of course, but not in iambics either – because Menander's thematic goal and structural plan had no place for such emphasis on the defiance of legitimate paternal concern for the family. The slave would have been brought up short in his deception, but the main focus of Menander would have been on the wayward son Sostratos. Although I believe that is a reasonable conjectural account of the way Menander would have restrained the operation of Syros as rogue, it cannot now be proved. Let us, then, go on to the early intrigue-comedies of Plautus, to see how he started off.

Two very early Plautine plays, which operate with intrigue, can serve as useful examples of the beginnings of 'heroic badness.' They are the *Ass Comedy* and *Braggart Soldier*. In the first, a young man needs money for a prostitute – the basic situation – and two household slaves take part in a plot of deception that swindles the mistress of money owed her for an ass. Once the swindle has succeeded, they control the finances for a while and are given a long scene in which they act out their exultation triumphantly, in order to demonstrate dramatically for the Roman audience their superiority.[17] However, Plautus allows them to play no part in the dénouement of the comedy, and it is evident that he devised the slaves' moment of triumph as an episodic comic effect, not as a central thematic statement. In fact, the slaves did not really make the decision to help the young lover, or even carry through the plan of deception themselves: it was the idea of the father, who ordered them to proceed, and it was the father who performed the decisive deception that got the money. So when Plautus abandons his momentary delight with the impudent slaves, he comes back to the father, the archdeceiver. *The Ass Comedy*, then, shows a basically subordinate role for slave-rogues, in conformance with the Greek original, I think, and with the general reality of Roman social practices. They are not heroes, though bad enough, and they occupy a distinctly inferior role (except for a promising sequence) in the total comic structure.

The Braggart Soldier is generally considered to have been composed a few years after the *Ass Comedy*, and it shows further development of the promise for a rogue of heroic badness. The problem is once again the love of a helpless young man for a courtesan, and again the slave helps him gain his girl by ingenious deception. Plautus certainly expands the role of this slave, Palinurus, by contrast with the previous play, and shows *him* plotting and carrying out his tricks. However, the target of the deception is a fool and knave, the braggart soldier, who combines within him all the relevant negative values for Plautus and his audience: he is a boastful coward, he is rich, he has kidnapped the prostitute, and he has become the illegitimate second master of Palinurus. When Palinurus disobeys and deceives this master in the interests of his original master, the young lover, to recover the kidnapped girl, his actions are not anarchic, but contribute to restoration of order and love.

Moreover, the slave does not act without authority and numerous allies. His young master, like all such young lovers, is utterly helpless, but an older friend, at whose house he secretly is staying, proves energetic and supportive. He keeps urging Palinurus on, and he shares in the illegal moves of the deceptions, at his own risk, with an enthusiasm that delights us. Thus, with his cooperation, a common wall between his and the soldier's house is secretly opened up to allow clandestine meetings between the prostitute and her lover, his guest. Later, he offers his house as the place where the soldier will be trapped in supposed adultery (a hoax, since the woman who pretends to be a rich and dissatisfied wife is really a clever and compliant prostitute-friend of his, always ready for some fun). It is the witty old man who playfully attributes senatorial and military dignity to Palinurus.[18] The slave himself makes no such claims, and he has no scene of triumph and plays no part in the final humiliation of the soldier: that, again, is the amusing task of the old man. In short, Plautus does not yet develop the opportunity for the comic transvaluation of the 'bad slave' into the heroic, central character; Palinurus functions as but one of the majority who are dedicated to punishing the knavish soldier and restoring legitimate order. It is true that, as the slave leaves the soldier and the play, Plautus has the foolish man aptly climax his folly with these words: 'Before this happened, I always used to think he was the worst of slaves [*servum pessumum*]; now, I realize that he is entirely loyal to me,' (line 1374). But that is a momentary ironic joke. Acting, as he does, on the side of the angels, Palinurus cannot really be designated as either a person of exemplary badness (*malitia*) or one of heroic Roman manliness. It turns out, indeed, that Plautus displaces *malitia* in this comedy to the characters who really show wonderful verve as actors in the plots to dupe the soldier. The courtesans each get credit as an exemplar of clever badness that elicits the admiration of Palinurus and the old man and helps out the weak young lover (cf. lines 188 and 887). Indeed, their action against the soldier becomes a competition of female badness (*conlatio malitiarum*, line 942).

A decade later, Plautus, at mid-career, had developed many possibilities of heroic badness. In *The Haunted House*, the slave Tranio clearly functions as the central character throughout the play, and the wonderfully improvised deceptions that he contrives to get money for his young master from the father are anarchic and like the heroic badness quite literally explored in later comedies. He is allowed to boast of his achievements as on a par with those of Alexander the Great (three iambic lines, 775–7), and he calls a 'senatorial session' of his supporters, but just as the plot is about to collapse, to make its ending more comic, not to magnify its beginning (line 1049). And, indeed, the plot fails, as we know from the start it must: Tranio takes refuge on the altar from his older master, who is furiously intent on punishing him, and only the intervention of an outsider buys the old man off from his fury and leaves Tranio for another day. Thus, the would-be hero is reduced to his proper role, and the father, though mocked and cheated, regains his authority.

The next step for Plautus is to allow the slave's badness complete success and to leave him heroically in power in the final scene. Examples of that fantastic scheme are two comedies composed in the late 190s, *Pseudolus* and *Epidicus*. For many readers today, Pseudolus is the quintessence of Plautine comic invention, and I would certainly want to view him as an exemplar of heroic badness.[19] He is the most self-conscious of any clever Plautine slave, so he constantly calls attention, with impudent pride, to his badness, to the incredible way he undertakes superhuman tasks and then accomplishes them. He humiliates his older master, Simo (though he does not actually defraud him), and he cheats a pimp of the price of a prostitute, who of course is desperately desired by the young master. The finale of the comedy has been composed as a lyric scene of drunken triumph, in which Pseudolus rubs his victory, impudently and with impunity, into the face of old Simo. The slave reels around the stage, burps familiarly at Simo, good-humouredly recites to him the victor's creed – 'woe to the defeated' (*vae victis* 1317) – and confidently styles himself as *vir malus*, smiling as the frustrated Simo calls him *pessumus homo* (line 1310). Admittedly, Plautus presents it as a moment of temporary victory, but it is total in the special comic representation.

Epidicus similarly scores a triumph over his outraged master, and he has the pleasure of turning the tables on angry Periphanes in the finale, so as to outwit his fury and to convert it into such total compliance and abject gratitude that the old man frees him on the spot. Thus, Epidicus' wits have enabled him to escape permanently from his slave role as 'worst of men.' The epilogue puts it all in a nutshell: 'Here is a man who has gained his liberty by his badness,' (*hic is homo est qui libertatem malitia invenit sua*, line 732). The slave has been able to nullify his master's anger because, in the course of supporting his young master's double love affair and of cheating Periphanes out of the price of two girls, he has accidentally bought to freedom a long-lost daughter of the old man. Learning of his lucky work before Periphanes does, he can then pose as having planned this noble deed and piously claim the reward of freedom: that is true heroic badness![20]

Some five years later, Plautus staged *The Bacchis-Sisters*, which builds the slave Chrysalus up into a superlative epic hero of badness and gives him the perfect triumph song. Up to that point late in Act IV, we might have expected that Plautus was taking the slave of Menander's *Double-Deceiver* and turning him into another Pseudolus or Epidicus. But he deliberately stops short, abandons Chrysalus to his celebrations off stage, and refocuses his and the audience's attention on the courtesan sisters. Chrysalus has, it seems, gone as far as he can on his own, and he faces inevitable and painful reality – his master's rightful anger – unless someone can intercede for him (as for Tranio). As I said earlier, I believe that Menander did let the father restore order and authority in his threatened home, bringing Sostratos and slave Syros to heel. Plautus, however, lets the Bacchis-sisters take over the play, which thereby changes its title aptly, and the forces of badness, domestic irresponsibility, social anarchy, and sensual pleasure completely prevail, to the humiliation of paternal respect and family honour.[21]

The changes that Plautus made to Menander's play and to his own highly successful characterization of the heroic rogue-slave, by shifting the emphasis and title from the slave-deceiver to the artful courtesans, suggest that the line of development of heroic badness has still not reached its conclusion in Plautine comedy. The triumphant slave is but a phase in a longer, more ingenious scheme. As I noted in the case of *The Braggart Soldier*, Palinurus the slave cannot work his schemes without the help of an energetic older man and a pair of witty, enterprising courtesans; and Plautus applies to them what is for him a praise-worthy term, *malitia*. Similarly, Chrysalus may exult in his reputation as 'a bad one' (line 783), but it is Bacchis who talks of her *malitia* (line 54) at the beginning of the play and accordingly seems to prepare us for Plautus' new emphasis.[22]

In Menander, if it is thematically necessary for the impudent slave to submit at the end to the older master's wise authority so that the home and family may operate under an intelligible hierarchy, it is even more necessary for the prostitute to yield to the interests of the family. Her erotic attractions and the money she demands of young lovers threaten the family, for she diverts the young master from taking a responsible role as husband of a suitable woman, father of the next generation, and careful steward of the family fortune. But Plautus does not treat the family as the essential measure of value for his comedy, and so, though he recognizes the stereotype of the 'bad prostitute' (*mala meretrix*: *Captivi*, line 57), he tends to change her character from that of negative menace to one of positive appeal: her 'badness' becomes the basis for her superiority to the male characters who share the stage with her. The Bacchis-sisters seduce the two young men; then, when the fathers of the young men storm over to the sisters' house to drag away the boys and Chrysalus, the sisters seduce the ridiculous old men. In Plautus' comic world, the appeal of sex, wine, and food is infinitely preferable to that of domesticity, and the Bacchis-sisters must dominate the old men and implicitly emerge as 'heroic.'

Among Plautus' last comedies are the *Truculent Man* and *Casina*. The former takes the theme of the masterful courtesan to a point where the comedy turns – for Plautus – unusually satiric.[23] The woman, suggestively named Phronesium (perhaps best translated as 'Prudence'), juggles with great skill and profit to herself, as I described in chapter 3, three simultaneous affairs. Not one of the three men earns our respect. However, the character of Phronesium herself causes problems for readers of Plautus, for, while she is manifestly superior in wit and *malitia* to her three victims, she acts only from selfish motives and does not exhibit the usual Plautine roguish qualities of verbal wit, physical energy, and good-humoured self-importance that combine to win over the audience.

Plautus assigns her one lyric monody early in the play (lines 448 ff), but does not let her bewitch us by the performance. Phronesium lacks the flamboyance and fantastic attractions of the rogue-slave, and her imagery does not move her into the world of Roman politics or heroic myth: she is a predatory creature. She has no senate, no army of supporters, no enemy to defeat for the public good; instead, her lover becomes metaphorically like an enemy city, full of plunder (line 170). In the inflexible world of Plautine Rome, a prostitute could not hope to escape her cruel conditions and become rich enough to settle down in dignity and be socially eligible, because of wealth, for respectability and even marriage. So Plautus could not fantasize

very far with the success of Phronesium. She remains a somewhat depressing example of a certain kind of *malitia*, no heroine, but demonstrably better than all three men with whom she
is involved.

For a more appealing portrait of woman's badness (*muliebris
malitia*), we need to turn to the last surviving Plautine comedy,
Casina. As Plautus organizes the plot, there are no prostitutes
and no young lovers; he uses two slaves, who appear strictly
subordinate to their owners, one to the husband and the other to
the wife.[24] The husband, Lysidamus, starts off as the would-be
rogue: he has a plot to fool his wife and, by using the cover of his
servant's marriage with an attractive housemaid, to sleep with
the maid himself the first night. Cleustrata, the wife, instinc-
tively opposes the marriage, because she claims it as her right to
dispose of the maid from her area of domestic responsibility. As
we saw, Diphilos and Plautus solved this marital dispute dramatically by the brilliant scene of the lot drawing, which gave
Diphilos' (and, perhaps originally, Plautus') comedy its title.
Cleustrata loses, and her roguish husband seems to have scored
a complete victory. Then, when she discovers the real purpose
and the extent of her husband's perfidy, she sets out energetically
and maliciously (if you want) to frustrate his plans and to humiliate him so openly that he will have to crawl back home and
behave in the future. She now pre-empts the role of rogue, and
the victory with it. In this scheme, the wife stands on the side of
good sense and marital fidelity, whereas the husband behaves
like an adolescent, and his dishonesty and false acting are both
ridiculous and highly punishable. In his frustration, the husband
and his caretaker accuse Cleustrata and her supporters of being
'bad stuff' (*mala res*, line 228), 'bad merchandise' (*mala merces*,
line 754), and the worst kind of trickster (line 645). They mean
what they say as pejorative, but Plautus invites us to take the
terms otherwise, because he has inclined us to view the women's
side as 'better.'

Cleustrata, then, develops a clever series of frustrating devices
by which her husband is fooled and the audience entertained. In
this respect, she removes herself far away from the merely mercenary tricks of Phronesium. She does not even resemble the

usual angry wife (e.g., in *The Ass Comedy*), who is concerned to protect her property as well as to punish her husband; Cleustrata does not have a large dowry, and her interest is in reordering the wayward household with the greatest number of laughs at her guilty husband. The key word for her activity is the Latin *ludi*, which refers to games, play, and stage performances. She 'plays games' (*ludificem*, line 560; *ludi ludificabiles*, line 761) with her husband, and she 'stages plays' (*ludos nuptialis*, line 856) for the audience. First, she acts the innocent herself and interferes with plans to make an empty house available for her husband's 'first night.' Then, she sends out a clever servant, Pardalisca, to act out a scene from tragedy, to terrify her husband with the story that Casina, like the operatic Lucia di Lammermoor, has gone crazy and is wielding a murderous sword and looking for him (lines 620 ff). And, finally, she organizes a comic performance, at which she as well as we are a laughing audience, where her husband goes to bed with her brawny slave (who is disguised as the bride Casina, of all things) and gets a bad beating for his lust, then rushes out in a state of considerable disrepair and publicly admits his disgrace. This is a special kind of triumph, and Cleustrata's 'badness' is also special. Neither a senator nor a victorious general in metaphorical terms (positions about which Plautus entertains some ambiguity), she is a creative artist, a veritable 'poet' (line 861), and that is probably the highest accolade that the poet Plautus can award to anyone.

In this chapter, I have attempted to describe the principal features of a special Plautine character, on whom he concentrates his comic attention: a rogue, male or female. Tracing Plautus' development of the rogue, I have shown how he starts tentatively with an uppity slave (*servus malus*) and, in successive plays, expands him into a superlative type, the worst of slaves (*servus pessimus*), a pyrotechnical scamp who can wrest freedom as well as gold from his angry, avaricious master. The Plautine rogue can also be female. She shows up supporting deception as a kind of 'wicked witch' or 'blasted bitch' (*mala meretrix*) among the courtesans of the early comedies, then develops to become the title character of *The Bacchis-Sisters* and almost the demonic principal of *The Truculent Man*. In his last play, *Casina*, Plautus heroizes the wittily independent wife Cleustrata (whom her scoundrel-husband considers *mala mulier* because she frustrates his infidelity). The question that still remains is: what does this comic 'heroization' of badness mean for Plautus' Roman audience? That is the subject of my final chapter.

Words, Numbers, Movement: Plautus' Mastery of Comic Language, Metre, and Staging

No anecdote or document survives that allows us to hear the words of Plautus or Terence speaking about himself or his craft. By sheer chance, diligent Plutarch reports for us a statement of Menander about his concept of dramatic composition, then interprets it for us. As the Athenian festival was approaching for which Menander was supposed to produce a comedy, and there was no sign of the play, he was asked when it would be done. Menander supposedly answered: 'By god, I *have* completed the comedy: I have worked out the plot; now, I need only fit the verses to that.' Plutarch comments: 'Clearly, he regarded the events as more necesssary and important than the words.'[1] It is, of course, risky to make too much of a statement like this. Normally, scholars have cited it as evidence of the extraordinary care with which Menander composed his intricate plots and pursued his delicate themes. Inheriting a tradition that Aristotle, too, shares – that plot takes priority over all other features of drama[2] – Menander emerges as the ideal exponent of that doctrine in Greek comedy. Nevertheless, although we must agree that the anecdote and Plutarch concentrate on plot, it is legitimate to utilize also Plutarch's reference to what was supposedly secondary to Menander, namely, words. Words, it seems, functioned subordinately in support of the general dramatic conception (plot and theme).

The dramatic mastery of Menander has emerged even more convincingly during this century, as papyrus finds have given us more and more of his words, in their dramatic contexts. We can

understand what Plutarch means when he attributes to the playwright the conviction that words stood in service to plot. It is
not that Menander just verbalized a scheme, as seems the case
today with many romantic novels and TV situation comedies. The
words of individual characters and of dialogue function effectively to capture the meaning and feeling of each situation and
to move the drama towards its planned conclusion. Many of
Menander's passages were excerpted in late antiquity and anthologized by men like Stobaeus, to serve as moralistic quotes in
sermons and other speeches, but that practice in no way proves
that Menander planned them as quotable excerpts, mere vehicles
of an ethical theme rather than of a character's experience. Where
we have recovered the context of such anthologized passages,
we can often recognize the delicate irony that qualifies the seeming assurance of the moralization. The readiest moralizer in
Menander, I calculate, is the slave. Although Menander invited
his audience to be generous towards slaves, who normally display great loyalty to their household and personal concern for
their masters, young and old, still he expected their moral 'wisdom' to be greeted with a certain smiling tolerance, not the total
acceptance for which later sermonizers employed it.

Menander's superb comic art illustrates one kind of comedy,
and his subordination of words and lines to the overall dramatic
conception constitutes a marvellous, but not the only, way of
working out a successful play. After all, the entire drama was
the unified conception of Menander, and the words were, indeed,
part of the plan, even if they might be said to have come after it.
Many writers would admit that, no matter how elaborate a plan
has been made first, the actual writing, putting the plan into
words, introduces significant changes into the original scheme,
so that, in a certain sense, the final plan depends signficantly on
the words. Plautus' situation and practices, to say nothing of his
views of comedy, differed strikingly from those of Menander and
the other great Greek comic artists whose plays he used. He was
working from another's comic composition, to which he could
show as much fidelity as he chose. But since mere translation
and strict adaptation were not Plautine ideals, since the plays
which he borrowed did not match his or his audience's comic

tastes, the words that appear in the Latin comedies do not work out the original Greek conception, nicely integrated into a meaningful melodrama, but they often stand out by themselves, to convey Plautus' disagreement with his Greek source and that Greek view of comedy, to demonstrate the sheer pleasure of words over plot, to suggest that verbal mastery (and the practical skill that such mastery implies) is far more appealing and comically attractive than a lot of seemingly trite romantic moralism. Granted, Plautus' audience did not understand or appreciate the delicate aspects of Menandrian art; but they had an entirely valid sense of an alternative kind of comedy, where words assumed greater importance, and Plautus knew how to produce those words. In this chapter, I review some of the ways in which the Latin poet made his words – in themselves, in their metrical setting, and in the comic action – function to create a comedy to be savoured by mouth and ear and eye more than by heart and brain.

Comedy by Words

Plautus establishes the verbal quality of his comedy in the opening words, whether of the prologue or, where that is delayed or abandoned, in the first scene. He and his characters, he shows, conduct a dialogue with the Greek originals and a conversation with the audience. For example, consider the start of *Mercator*:

> *duas res simul nunc agere decretumst mihi:*
> *et argumentum et meos amores eloquar.*
> *non ego item facio ut alios in comoediis*
> *vi vidi amoris facere, qui aut Nocti aut Dii*
> *aut Soli aut Lunae miserias narrant suas:*
> *quos pol ego credo humanas querimonias*
> *non tanti facere, quid velint, quid non velint;*
> *vobis narrabo potius meas nunc miserias.* (lines 1–8)

[I have decided to do two things simultaneously now: I shall explain both the background and my love-life. I am not doing as I have seen others in comedies doing under the power of love, who

set forth their wretchedness either to Night or Day or Sun or
Moon: who I definitely do not believe make much account of
human complaints, what they might wish or not wish; I shall
set forth rather to *you* now my wretchedness.]

The speaker is the young lover Charinus, who in the remainder of the play shows no particular understanding of himself or
the comic genre. Here, he carefully analyses his behaviour and
compares it with that of other comic lovers: they complain to
the elements; he is going to address the audience. I consider this
a deliberate intrusion by Plautus (not in the original Greek of
Philemon) to force into the open the artificiality of the prologue
and of the convention of apostrophizing aspects of Nature. Lines
3–8 break the dramatic illusion and, in rejecting as ridiculous
one apostrophe, announce a different apostrophe to the audience, which would be problematic, too, except that Plautus intends to maintain his relationship with the audience throughout
the course of this comedy. After all, when the lover apostrophizes
the Night or the Moon – it is doubtful that the list should include
Day and Sun, except to suit the Latin love of words – what is he
doing except indirectly addressing the audience? But when he
does appeal to these elements of Nature, at least he seems to
have a reason, namely, to ask for help; whereas addressing the
audience accomplishes nothing within the dramatic frame, but
wins attention for the play. Charinus declares his agnosticism in
lines 6–7, further exposing his and Plautus' superiority to dramatic
conventions of naturalism. In short, Plautus has used Charinus
here as anything but the foolish, totally love-possessed young
man he should be: he serves, rather, the Roman writer's purpose
of wrecking the prologue and creating a connection with the
audience apart from the drama.

Charinus does not exhibit any striking vocabulary, but he does
show a fondness for words, repeating *facere* in lines 3 and 4, giving four 'deities' in a list connected with the polysyndeton of
aut, repeating in line 7 *quid velint* in positive and negative form,
and echoing *miserias narrant suas* + dative of line 5 at line 8.
Now, after briefly identifying the Greek and Roman titles and
writers of the comedy (lines 9–10), he starts on his story of love.

In three lines, he quickly narrates how he went as trader to Rhodes and fell in love with an extraordinarily beautiful woman. But then he turns back to the audience (lines 14–15) to request its gracious attention. Note the potential contradiction here: Charinus has projected no personal character so far and thus earned no sympathy for his dramatic role or his love; yet as prologue speaker, playing with his opportunity to be within and outside the drama, he has aroused our interest.

In line 16, Charinus once again seems to distinguish himself from the usual lovers of comedy, but line 17, in which he might have clarified that distinction, has come down to us hopelessly corrupt. Then, he continues with a list of the faults that attend love (lines 18–23). Not content with that list, he proceeds to expand its contents with twenty-one more items, ending with *multiloquium, parumloquium* (lines 24–31). Both these Latin words seem to have been invented by Plautus here. The first captures our feelings about the verbosity of Charinus' lists and speech in general, and indeed he will soon (line 37) ask the audience not be be angered by his wordiness. The second serves as a surprise joke by which Plautus lets Charinus make fun of himself. What he calls 'brevity' or 'speaking in a few words' (*pauciloquium*, line 34: another neologism) turns out to be the lover's failure to be usefully eloquent for his suit (lines 35–6). But that kind of 'brevity' has fuelled his verbosity now for more than twenty lines and postponed the promised *argumentum*, which he started momentarily at line 11. Finally, at line 40 he resumes his sketch of the background and holds himself to it for the next sixty lines, until he comes back to the beautiful Rhodian woman he earlier mentioned. After telling us enough about her to indicate that she was a slave-prostitute and that he spent a night with her, he affects to come quickly to the point: 'What need for words? I bought her and yesterday brought her here [to Athens]. I don't want my father to know that' (lines 106–7). In that query, *quid verbis opus est?*, Charinus for the first time seems to consult brevity. But it is significant that he chooses to shorten the background narrative, whereas he has greatly expanded the 'business' with the audience and his 'dialogue' with the Greek play Plautus has adapted. Although this is not Plautus' longest prologue, it surpasses in length anything that we know from Menander.[3]

The verbosity of Charinus, then, does not enhance his status as a character or enrich the dramatic power of the play; on the contrary, it creates an alliance between Charinus (who, by stepping outside his role, becomes a spokesman for Plautus) and the audience to stand apart and withhold sympathy from the Greek characters and composition of Philemon. In the course of Plautus' adapted comedy, Charinus continues to waste the sympathy that, I think certain, the Greek playwright generated for him.[4] Instead of conveying some genuine feeling about his father, his Rhodian beloved, and his loyal friend Eutychus, he is made by Plautus to emote and rant and rage in the most extreme and extravagant manner. His two big scenes with Eutychus – first, when his friend reports the bad news that the girl has been taken away (lines 588 ff) and, second, when his friend tries to get him to be reasonable about seeing the girl who has been located (lines 842 ff), but cannot be approached just yet – give him the opportunity to overact, to overstate his misery, and thus to make himself ridiculous to the audience. Here are some of his responses to Eutychus in lines 601 ff: 'Before you catch your breath, tell me in a single word: Where am I: here in life or among the dead? [Notice his impossible demand for an answer in one word, after all his loquacity.] ... I am dead; that statement has killed me ... Eutychus, you are committing a capital crime ... You have plunged your sword into my throat; now I shall fall dead ... Now you are hurling mountains of blazing evil against me. Go on, torment me, executioner, once you have begun.' Ringing the changes on various metaphors of death, Charinus keeps saying that he is dead and dying, but of course remains very much alive – comically so. The more he varies his images, the less credible he becomes. Thus, by expanding what may have been a single metaphor in the original, Plautus undoes the melodrama of the Greek.

Charinus is the most talkative character in his comedy, but Plautus uses his wordiness to make him an exaggerated and silly figure. As the typical lover, he cannot control his situation, and so his words emphasize his helplessness. Nevertheless, in the often spectacular imagery and ranting speeches that Plautus assigns him, Charinus has the premier role. We laugh at him, but we enjoy his verbiage, and the play acquires its unique Plautine character largely because of this talkative and silly lover.

In plays of Plautus' maturity, drastic changes are introduced to inherited love stories, and the typical lover gets shunted aside, upstaged by more enterprising characters who can act out Plautus' concept of comic heroism. These heroes revel in language; they are supremely articulate and love to use words to deceive and to boast of their exploits. Nothing like this has come down to us in Greek New Comedy, and the conclusion seems unassailable, that Plautus has introduced these verbal magicians and their boasting routines into his adaptations. In the *Mostellaria*, the lover Philolaches attracts much attention at the start, and he briefly stars in a lyric aria (lines 84–156), but by line 405 he has declared himself a client of his slave Tranio and yielded the stage to him for the rest of the play, and Tranio assumes the lead as the intrepid rogue. With one false story after another, he leads his master, the neighbour, and a loanshark a merry chase, doing it all with words, nothing more. In themselves, the lies are spectacular, and Tranio draws them out for our amusement, making his victims ridiculous. At one point, Plautus has him turn to the audience and chortle over his heroism and the folly of the others:

> *Alexandrum magnum atque Agathoclem aiunt maxumas*
> *duo res gessisse: quid mihi fiet tertio,*
> *qui solus facio facinora inmortalia?*
> *vehit hic clitellas, vehit hic autem alter senex.*
> *novicium mihi quaestum institui non malum:*
> *nam muliones mulos clitellarios*
> *habent, at ego habeo homines clitellarios.*
> *magni sunt oneris: quidquid imponas vehunt.* (lines 775–82)

[They say that two men, Alexander the Great and Agathocles performed the greatest deeds. What about me as a third, who single-handed do deeds that are deathless? This old man here carries saddle bags, and this man does, too. I have invented for myself a new means of profit that's not bad at all: muleteers

have mules carrying saddle bags, but I have human beings to
carry them. They are great beasts of burden: they'll carry
whatever you load on them.]

Tranio here speaks behind his victims' backs, as he walks
from one to the other, addressing us, calling our attention to his
power and magnificent status. First, he links Alexander the Great,
unquestionably a monumental figure, and Agathocles of Sicily,
perhaps more familiar to his audience, but also of lesser stature.
That might prepare us for the anticlimax of his claim to be a
third 'hero,' because of his 'immortal and single-handed feats.'
Then, instead of elaborating the military imagery, as other slave-
rogues in Plautus often do, Tranio is made to emphasize the
anticlimax by his sudden switch of images. His victims are not
brave foes in battle (like those of Alexander and Agathocles), but
human pack-animals; and his glorious achievement consists in
outdoing conventional muleteers, who depend on mules! Thus,
Plautus lets us enjoy Tranio's proud boasts, but also distance
ourselves from his limited heroic horizons, as he tries to pull
down the greatest generals to his level, whose proud image is
that of a drover of old men.

Plautus finds it very easy to contrive grandiloquent and ranting
soliloquies for his characters, both his heroes and his villains.
Ballio the pimp, in *Pseudolus*, has a wonderful part; and other
pimps and many fathers, when they have been cheated and made
fools of, get some superb comic speeches to express their angry
frustration. Euclio, the miser of *Aulularia*, takes over the comedy, almost entirely eclipsing the lover, Lyconides, and the love
plot involving his daughter. He is Plautus' best comic 'villain'
because of his torrent of excited, image-filled words and his vol-
canic energy racing around the stage. However, Plautus does not
confine his verbal magic to soliloquies: he creates many scenes
of verbal interchange, where words, not dramatic theme, dominate his interest and the audience's attention.

Midway through the *Bacchides*, as Chrysalus starts to recover
from his young master's folly in returning the stolen money and
prepares to cheat his old master again of the sum, Plautus stages
his confrontation with old Nicobulus as follows: Nicobulus be-

lieves he is able to out-think the slave and his planned deception, and he scornfully taunts him, but Chrysalus taunts him
right back and totally out-talks and -thinks him.

> NIC. *propterea hoc facio ut suadeas gnato meo*
> *ut pergraecetur tecum, terven*e*fice.*
> CHRYS *o stulte, stulte, nescis nunc venire te;*
> *atque in eopse astas lapide, ut praeco praedicat.*
> N. *responde: quis me vendit? C. quem di diligunt,*
> *adulescens moritur, dum valet, sentit, sapit.*
> *hunc si ullus deus amaret, plus annis decem,*
> *plus iam viginti mortuom esse oportuit:*
> *terrai iam odium ambulat, iam nil sapit*
> *nec sentit, tantist quantist fungus putidus.* (lines 812–21)

[N. I am doing this precisely so that you can persuade my son
to join you in Greek perversion, you triple villain.
C. You poor, poor fool: you don't even realize that you're up for
sale now. You're standing on the very block, as the auctioneer
starts to announce the proceedings.
N. Tell me, who's selling me?
C. 'Those whom the gods love die young,' at the peak of health,
sensibility, and intelligence. If any god loved this man [pointing
Simo out to the audience], he should have died more than ten,
no, more than twenty years ago. Now he walks about, loathed
by every person on earth, devoid of intelligence, devoid of
sensibility, worth about as much as a rotten mushroom.]

Nicobulus expresses his contempt for his slave by his sardonic
tone and by the choice of verb and epithet in the second line: the
verb, with its chauvinistic view of Greek depravity, could not, of
course, have been in Menander's text, and we know that the
epithet is unique here, hence also introduced by Plautus. Literally, it means 'triple-poisoner' and specifies Chrysalus' supposed
villainy in a highly picturesque manner. Nicobulus implicitly
wishes to execute this 'hardened criminal.' Undisturbed, however,
by his master's confident irony, Chrysalus taunts him with his
weakness and ignorance. He starts with the metaphor of a slave

auction and claims that, unwittingly, Nicobulus is on the block, up for sale. This image points to a role reversal, and Nicobulus asks the obvious question: who has the power to sell him? Although Chrysalus does not deign to answer him, we can understand (and this scene confirms the fact) that Chrysalus now has assumed mastery over foolish, gullible Nicobulus, a mastery that largely depends on his verbal superiority. By way of answer, the slave quotes a famous saying, which should serve as a consolation to parents of prematurely dead children: the gods take young men away when they love them and wish to spare them the misfortunes and misery of later life.[5] We know that Menander used this saying, too, since he quoted it as a single trimeter, but his line comes down to us entirely divorced from its context, to frustrate any attempt to ascertain how it worked in the Greek comedy. I suspect that the way Plautus has divided the saying over two half-lines indicates his tactics of expansion and comic articulation. What may have been adequate for Menandrian irony in a single line, becomes, in Plautus' Latin, the basis for a highly amusing tricolon of interpretation. After analysing human life into health, feeling, and intelligence, Chrysalus proceeds to apply the tricolon in reverse order to his master, who lacks intelligence and feeling, he asserts, and has as much 'health' as a rotten fungus.

Thus, the slave has retorted to Nicobulus' confident insults with three distinct sequences of verbal mastery. Of these, I believe, only the saying about dying young was in Menander: Plautus has introduced both the image of the slave auction and the caustic elaboration of the Greek saying, which ends by reducing the master to a disgustingly decayed mushroom. To this, Nicobulus has no answer. Almost speechless in his anger, he commands that Chrysalus be dragged off and lashed to a column, to await further punishment. Slaves do not challenge their masters in this impudent manner in Menander; Plautus has created this kind of verbal confrontation, to give symbolic victory and 'mastery' to the articulate rogue. When, in line 818, Chrysalus stopped addressing Nicobulus directly and switched to the third person, he implicity, probably explicitly, was addressing the audience and gesturing scornfully at 'this man' Nicobulus. It is

Plautus' typical technique of letting his hero speak in his role and simultaneously comment on his performance for our delight. Thus, the words are mostly Plautine, not Menandrian here.

Critics often note the abundance of Plautine diction, especially in relation to the dictions of Menander and Terence. Plautine theatre makes lavish use of words: striking neologisms that exploit length and resonance, like *tervenefice* above; picturesque images, like being on the block or resembling a rotten fungus; series of verbs or nouns, in asyndeton or polysyndeton; wonderful stretches of alliteration and assonance that emphasize a key comic idea; resonant and significant names that substitute ridiculous overtones for the conventional Greek names of the originals, such as Pistoclerus and Mnesilochus for the two young men (originally Moschos and Sostratos) in the *Bacchides*. It takes normal situations of excitement, anger, despair, enthusiasm, which Menander and Terence keep strictly under control and subordinate to their dramatic themes, and they become occasions for histrionic performances, cameo parts for actors that use comedy to generate laughs. Terence will not let the 'running slave' (*servus currens*) take off and perform the glorious routine that Plautus leads us joyously to expect. Terence will not even let the angry father voice his rage in a long, satisfying rant against son and slave: all he is permitted to do is to say that he can barely control himself because of wrath, and then he quickly simmers down and takes rational steps to deal with the situation.[6] Plautus wants us to enjoy and laugh at all kinds of energetic excitement and to distance ourselves from them, relishing them as performance. The more words he uses, the more he elaborates routines and situations, the less we identify with the supposedly deep passions that lie behind these great 'acts,' the more we let ourselves just go with the flow of words and the verbal mastery that dominates.

Menander's characters seem to be straining to understand what it means to be a human being: they must learn to think, feel, and talk humanely, in order to live properly as men and women. It is significant that Cnemon, the 'inhuman human being,' lets his rage get out of hand at first, and Menander can give him an opening speech in which he indulges his wild misanthropy by wishing he had the Gorgon's Head of Perseus, so that he could turn all mankind into silent statues. He must be 'humanized' during the play, to tone down his own speech and to accept the ordinary talk of his relatives and neighbours. In Plautus, however, we find an emphasis on the inhuman and the superhuman, and the extraordinary words he assigns his characters turn average situations – situations that his Greek sources kept in control to serve the humane theme – into fantastic, wildly unreal and hence thoroughly enjoyable scenes for the audience. If speech is the definitive feature of humankind, wildly improbable speech defines the comic beings that Plautus renders larger than life. And no small part of that largeness and grandiloquence is the versatile metre in which he embodies his words.

Comedy by the Numbers

According to Aulus Gellius, Plautus composed before his death the epitaph he wanted engraved on his monument. It declared that, when he died, Comedy itself went into mourning, and those special features of his style, which perished with him – namely, Laughter, Play, Jesting, and numberless Numbers[7] – wept inconsolably. Less than two hundred years later, Horace produced a very different judgment on Plautus and his salient qualities. Far from being the beloved of Comedy, Plautus emerges in Horace's version as the favourite of the stupid, benighted Roman public of the late third and early second centuries, who indeed praised both his numbers and his witticisms, but 'admired both elements all too tolerantly, not to say stupidly.'[8] We have already discussed some aspects of Plautine wit as it resides in the words he assigns to his energetic and articulate characters, enough to show that neither Plautus nor his contemporary audiences were stupid to exploit and praise this kind of diction. Horace seems to have let the purist notions for which he was fighting in Augustan times blind him to the true merits of Plautine comic language, and the efforts Horace had also made to refine the metrical practices of Catullus and his generation seem to have hardened him against the special genius of Plautus as comic metrician. I wish now to put that metrical achievement in the proper perspective, to show how Plautus, in exploring the possibilities of 'numberless numbers,' gave to Roman New Comedy a unique quality, which, alas, failed to survive him and should be mourned.

Menander and other Greek writers of New Comedy had no desire to try out the merits of many numbers, that is, polymetry, and consequently their plays are devoid of lyric and songs. After all, Greek Comedy had steadily reduced the amount and range of its metres since the Old Comedy of Aristophanes and the fifth century, abandoning the excitement and variety, first, of the parabasis and agon and, then, of the chorus itself (at least as an integral actor in the comedy). Although the papyri of the two virtually complete Menandrian plays that have survived indicate the point in the text for four choral performances per play, between the acts (but not apparently at the end of the play, either by way of final comment or as part of the festive exit of the actors from the stage), the indication consists simply of the word 'chorus,' in the genitive case, and the word on which that genitive depended remains unclear. It might have been 'dance' or 'song,' but the absence of a verbal text for the choruses implies that, if verbal, they were not regarded as very necessary to the play's composition and very possibly not even composed by the playwright; if the choruses were only dance, they were a minor interlude that again was left up to a choreographer rather than prescribed by the poet. At the end of Act I, where that section survives in Menander's papyri, we regularly find an announcement of the chorus' entrance; none of the other choral interludes receives any notice from the comic text. What we find there in Act I proves very dismaying for any modern revivals of the plays, because the last speaker says that he sees some drunken revellers approaching, and therefore he advises that he and his companion(s) should withdraw and avoid contact and difficulty with this inebriated group. Without a written text to specify what the chorus said or did, directors of revivals today feel obliged to stage some kind of drunken dance, with or without words or incoherent sounds. Presumably, Menander and Athenian theatre did make some pleasant use of this convention, but we cannot today determine its dramatic utility or metrical nature, and we tend to agree with the Roman decision to give up entirely on such extravagant and irrelevant choral passages and to stage the play continuously, without formal interludes and acts.

When we remove from consideration, then, the choral sections of Menandrian comedy, the choice of numbers becomes very purposefully small. Most Greek New Comedy functions as relatively serious, probable or realistic discussion by one, two, or three characters, and convention calls therefore for the predominant employment of the most prosaic of Greek metres, the iambic trimeter. Whether any play used iambics throughout cannot be demonstrated, but our statistics suggest that they averaged about 80 per cent of the total lines per play. In the two comedies that we can regard as virtually intact, Menander introduces a new metre in the fourth act, as he quickens the pace and emotional level of the dénouement: that metre is the trochaic tetrameter.[9] It provides the rhythm for the entire act of the *Samia* and for the last half of Act IV of the *Dyskolos* (emphasizing the powerful effect of falling down the well on Cnemon, the grouch). In both plays, then, Act V starts out again with the iambic trimeter, then switches midway to a second metre, to trochaic tetrameter again (*Samia*) or iambic tetrameter catalectic (*Dyskolos*), also to pick up the pace and end the comedy on an energetic rhythm. That, however, constitutes the limit of metrical enterprise in Menander. He made intelligent use of metre to support his composition; metre was never a comic element in itself, a technique for bravura performance and laughable histrionics. All individual aspects of his plays yielded priority to the unifying conception with which, after considerable forethought, he composed his comedies; metre could be no exception.

The Romans took over the three metres that Menander had employed, but they radically changed the proportions he had used, reducing the dominance of the iambic trimeter (slightly modified in Rome as a looser senarius) from 80 to about 53 per cent in Terence (his admirer and loyal adaptor) and only 30 per cent or less in some of Plautus' plays, increasing the ratio of the trochaic tetrameter (= septenarius), and using three long variants, not just the iambic tetrameter catalectic (= septenarius), but also a true eight-beat metre of iambics and trochaics, octonarii both.[10] These long variants for the senarius used a particular technique of performance: a flute accompanied them, and the actor recited them to the music. Thus, they constituted a special kind of dialogue or monologue, which the Romans called *canticum* in distinction from the prosaic, more ordinary level of discourse, called *diverbium*, used with unaccompanied senarii. If even Menander's admirer Terence rewrote iambic short lines as *cantica* and allowed himself nearly 50 per cent of 'musical' metres, compared with the Greek practice of using 20 per cent or less, it would appear that Plautus' flamboyant resort to music and lively metres, to go with his lively language, could not be ignored by even the most devout reaction towards the soberer methods of Greek comedy. Plautus' exploitation of metrical diversity, of musical accompaniment, of the heightened effects of longer lines, and finally of lyric metres made major contributions to the rhythm and auditory appeal of Roman comedy.

Plautus did not display his full metrical virtuosity in his earliest plays, and that fact suggests that he did not achieve his results simply by imitating older writers' practices. On the contrary, the evidence points to a growing mastery of the metrical and musical possibilities, which developed along with a growing independence from the Greek plays he was adapting, from the Greek conception of comedy that he was assimilating to the different kind of audience and sociopolitical context of Rome. What may be the earliest surviving Plautine comedy, the *Asinaria*, demonstrates that Plautus was determined from the beginning to cut drastically back on iambic senarii and write expansive longer lines that would be comically abundant and enjoy musical accompaniment. In a virtual reversal of Menandrian proportions, the play shows 22 per cent senarii; 78 per cent of the lines utilize six long sequences of trochaic septenarii, iambic octonarii, and iambic septenarii. With such proportions, it cannot be claimed that any one sequence of trochaics – there are three of them, for example – has a strikingly special effect (by comparison with Menander's deliberately sparing usage for the dénouement); but the prevalence of these and other long lines proves Plautus' disposition for rhythmical excitement or, to put it another way, for the comic exaggeration that can be enhanced by long metres and flute music.

Between lines 126 and 746, the *Asinaria* has no calm dialogue in senarii at all. In that space, the abundance and pulsating rhythm of trochaic and iambic septenarii allow the playwright to make fun of the plight of the young lover Argyrippus and to emphasize the tough wit of the bawd, then to show the two slaves running wild with the intrigue, both in planning and carrying it out against the gullible trader, and finally to stage a rollicking scene, expanded to have four speakers, in which the slaves humble Argyrippus and his girlfriend. One other short section seems to have been an experiment for Plautus that would prove the beginning of a major metrical development in future comedies. At his first appearance, the foolish young Argyrippus stands outside the closed doors of his courtesan's house, in the conventional pose of the excluded lover, angry and frustrated. Plautus has chosen to introduce this comic character with a sequence of jerky cretics, eleven lines of identical pattern that, because of their regularity, count rather as a variant of *canticum* than as lyric: *sicine hoc fit? foras aedibus me eici? | promerenti optume hoccin preti redditur? | bene merenti mala es, male merenti bona es.* (lines 127–9) –'Is that the way it is? Am I to be thrown out of the house? Is that the reward given to one who deserves the very best? You're bad to one who deserves good, good to one who deserves bad.' It may not look like much, but this is probably the tentative start of the extravagant lyric monodies that Plautus will assign young lovers at first entrance in coming years.

In two other plays, which Plautus wrote before he had developed his lyrical talents, he continued to utilize both the trochaic and iambic septenarii as the medium for lively scenes and to transform the calmer, more down-to-earth Greek language and rhythm of iambic trimeter into a more congenial vehicle, but he did not venture boldly far beyond. The *Miles* has more than two hundred lines in iambic septenarii, in three long sequences, but its only daring novelty consists of a skilful sequence in regular anapaestic tetrameter, which turns into a delight the encounter between the soldier and the woman who poses as the servant, herself totally infatuated, of the infatuated rich matron who seeks the love of Pyrgopolyneices.[11] The *Mercator*, except for one scene of iambic septenarii, reserved to introduce to us the winning ways of the courtesan Pasicompsa (lines 499–543), alternates iambic senarii and trochaic septenarii, giving significant preference to the more animated trochaic rhythm (492 lines versus 426); in addition, Plautus has devised a lachrymose soliloquy for Charinus to declaim that, by its artful mixture of bacchiac, anapaestic, and trochaic lines, closely approaches the versatility and effect of lyric monodies which will occur in every subsequent comedy.[12]

In the two remaining plays which Plautus wrote before the end of the third century, *Cistellaria* and *Stichus*, it is notable that he experimented with a lyric device that he did not adopt regularly thereafter: he opened the comedy with lyric conversation.[13] Since both plays derived from Menander, we know for a fact that the Roman song metres came from the calm iambic trimeters of the Greek. The title of Menander's original of the *Cistellaria* refers to the opening scene, which must have been strikingly successful: it featured three women lunching together and conversing intimately about the painful existence that faced a young courtesan who had tender feelings towards her first lover, in spite of the fact that he seemed to betray the typical infidelity of most men. Plautus, for the most part, uses the lyric to enhance the pathos of the young Selenium, not to make it silly; in other words, he emphasizes the sentimental quality of Menander's scene by his metrical medium, postponing his deconstructive tactics until later. He operated similarly with the opening lyric of *Stichus*, which is a dialogue between two unhappy sisters, whose husbands have been absent as traders for two whole years and who are now under pressure from their father to consider themselves widows and remarry. Because Plautus never seems to have undercut female roles as persistently and comically as those of males – later, he tends to adapt plays which feature silly male lovers and to avoid those where loving wives or courtesans appear – these plays, then, begin on a falsely sympathetic note; they never succeed, despite some raucous developments farther on, in establishing what we admire as the quintessential Plautine verve, of language, metre, and movement.

In *Stichus*, the slave Pinacium comes rushing in from the port, a typical *servus currens* bringing unusually good news, and his routine develops in long lines of iambic octonarii (274–308). After he briefly converses with the parasite, he proceeds to knock excitedly on the door, eager to deliver his news. Plautus modulates the octonarii during the knocking into anapaests. Thus, he did not depart from his limited numbers in that comedy, except in the flamboyant opening. In *Cistellaria*, by contrast, he proved capable of two other lyrical extravaganzas in addition to the opening tour de force. For the first entrance of the young man who plays the role of lover opposite Selenium, he creates a fine monody in anapaestic lines of varying extent (203 ff), which, after twenty-five verses, still continues as the archetype manuscript broke off in a sizeable lacuna. Alcesimarchus, the operatic performer, declares his supreme misery (like Charinus in the earlier more modest bacchiac-anapaestic passage of *Mercator*), but with an abundance of verbs, alliteration, and parallelism that turns him into an all-too-voluble travesty of Menander's sympathetic lover. Still farther on, Plautus commences the sequence for which his comedy earned its title, *The Comedy of the Casket*, by assigning the hobbling and querulous old servant, who has dropped the casket in the street, an anxious monody composed of anapaestic, bacchiac, and cretic lines in a skilfully comical pattern, designed to turn the search for a lost item into a ridiculously operatic hunt for the most precious treasure. Clearly, in the *Cistellaria*, Plautus has made giant strides towards the lyrical comedy that characterizes his plays of the 190s and 180s. He is now ready to reveal himself the master of 'numberless numbers.'

Plautus' favourite lyric metres are cretics, anapaests, and bacchiacs, but he also displays glyconics, dochmiacs, and Reizian cola, and he combines these various metres into songs of dazzling patterns. Probably, the most memorable songs are the monodies (or operatic 'arias'), which provide an actor a superb opportunity for a spectacular performance on entrance or at other key points in the comedy. We have seen how Plautus experimented with sentimental monodies for the pathetic females in the openings of *Stichus* and *Cistellaria*. Although he later abandoned the lyric beginning, Plautus developed a practice of using lyric in the first dramatic scene after sketching the background in senarii. In *Rudens*, the two girls who have been shipwrecked and come to shore after harrowing dangers both get sentimental monodies and then recount their terrors in lyric (lines 185 ff). That is a memorable entrance and introduction to the audience. Another character to whom Plautus likes to give an opportunity to emote on entrance is the helpless male lover: the trial passages with Argyrippus, Charinus, and Alcesimarchus eventuate in magniloquent and versatile 'arias' such as that of Toxilus (*Persa*, lines 1 ff), Lysiteles (*Trinummus*, lines 223 ff), and especially of Philolaches (*Mostellaria*, lines 84–153). In a series of bacchiacs and cretics, artfully punctuated by longer lines of iambic octonarii, Philolaches meditates on the *simulacrum* (line 89) of the life of man as a house, and the life of a lover as a sadly dilapidated house in a state of ill repair. What was a brief comparison at best in the Greek original, Plautus has let Philolaches spin out with verbose abundance that tends to undercut his penitence and make a mockery of his love, entirely in line with Plautus' programmatic ridicule and upstaging of amatory themes.

Since young lovers, male or female, did not necessarily have entrances in the Greek originals after the basic exposition, Plautus took what he had and turned almost anything into a lyric opportunity very early in the play. He regales us, for example, with the cowardly boasting of Sosia the slave (*Amphitruo*, lines 153 ff), the comically vicious power of Ballio giving orders to his prostitutes (*Pseudolus*, lines 133 ff), and the angry frustration of Menaechmus, who resents his wife and flees from her to Erotion (*Menaechmi*, lines 110 ff). Then, he turns ordinary iambic dialogues of the originals into lively operatic duos: in this fashion, he introduces the prisoners who will star in *Captivi* (lines 195 ff), and he plays with the conversation in which Eunomia suggests, to his total horror, that her brother Megadorus, a confirmed bachelor, get married (*Aulularia*, lines 120 ff). In the late plays *Truculentus* and *Casina*, the first lyrics feature interesting variants on the victimized woman and her sentimental song: Astaphium introduces herself as a predatory prostitute, wittily and impudently planning how to fleece her male customers, would-be exploiters of weak women (*Truculentus*, lines 95 ff); Cleustrata expresses her angry impatience with her husband and determination not to be a victim, as she complains to a neighbour woman of his behaviour (*Casina*, lines 144 ff). Thus, Plautus quickly establishes his comic tone through the lyrical extravaganzas that he assigns to a variety of characters, major and minor.

As he comes into his own, Plautus takes the artful composition of a Menander or other Greek source and exploits it as a scenario, from which he can take off freely with lyrical expansions (or, if you wish, digressions) that, like his other idiosyncratic alterations, transform the Greek play into a Plautine comedy. We can thus see that a highly restrained original with about 80 per cent prosaic iambic trimeters has not only yielded to his insistence on major amounts of *canticum*, but also inspired as many as five lyric performances, solos, duets, and even the equivalent of entire acts, such as the triumphant celebrations that provide the finales of *Persa* and *Pseudolus*, drunken orgies of slaves who have fooled confident pimps (and old Simo, too, in *Pseudolus*), mockingly staged as a travesty of a great Roman triumph.

English does not take kindly to exact translation of Plautine metres. A sequence of cretics or bacchiacs faces the translator with major difficulties, then strikes the audience as nearly incredible. Only the anapaestic patterns come easy to the English ear, which has heard similar patterns in Gilbert and Sullivan and other nineteenth-century poetry. However, it should be the obligation of every honest translation of Plautus to shape Plautine lyric passages into a metrical form which stands out as different from the sections of *diverbium* and *canticum*, even if it must resort to shorter lines of trochees or iambs, so that the special rhythmical lilt and the verbiage which it supports can have an appropriate effect. Let me conclude this chapter by looking closely at two lyrical monodies and the techniques that two modern translators employed to render them.

First, I consider one of many virtuoso performances of Pseudolus. The slave has just left the stage empty, after addressing the audience and announcing that he would be 'assembling in troop formations his sycophancies or Greek tricks' (*dum concenturio in corde sycophantias*, line 572). To pass the time, he invites them to listen to a flute player. Presumably, then, the flute music began to sound, as a kind of interlude at first, but then as the introduction for Pseudolus' sudden return in a totally ecstatic mood, jumping about in lyric after the iambic senarii and calmness with which he departed.

pro Iuppiter, ut mihi quidquid ago lepide omnia prospereque
eveniunt: [anap.]   575
neque quod dubitem neque quod timeam meo in pectore
conditumst consilium. [anap.]
nam ea stultitia est, facinus magnum timido cordi credere;
[anap.]
   nam omnes res perinde sunt [iamb.]
ut agas, ut eas magni facias; nam ego in meo pectore prius
[anap.]
   ita paravi copias, [troch.]
duplicis, triplicis dolos, perfidias, ut, ubiquomque hostibu'
congrediar [anap.]   580
(maiorum meum fretus virtute dicam, mea industria et malitia
fraudulenta), [bacch.]
facile ut vincam, facile ut spoliem meos perduellis meis
perfidiis. [anap.]
nunc inimicum ego hunc communem meum atque vostrorum
omnium [tr.]   585
Ballionem exballistabo lepide. [troch.]

I give Casson's translation of these eleven lines, which he has set up with a special typography to occupy an entire page:[14]

   Holy mackerel! It's marvelous! Everything I try [anap.]
     Works out just like a charm. [iamb.]

   Up in here is a scheme I can certify [anap.]
     Is guaranteed free of harm. [iamb.]

When your eye's on the big things, it's madness, I say, [anap.]
To proceed in a timid or half-hearted way. [anap.]   577

     The way that things work out [iamb.]
     Is completely up to you.

You want to do big things?
Then think and act big too!

You take *me*. Why, up here in this head, [anap.]
   Standing by for the fray,
Are my armies – plus ambush, intrigue,
   Dirty deals, and foul play.   580

With the courage inherited from a long line of heroes, [anap.]
 With the double-cross serving as shining shield,
The enemy's mine wherever I'll meet him –
I'll phony my foemen from the field!

   Just watch me now. I'm set to go, [iamb.]
   To fight the man who's our common foe,
   To rally-oh,
   And sally-oh
      'Gainst Ballio!   585

As can be seen from my annotations to the translation, Casson has preserved the predominantly anapaestic metre, which is lively and congenial to our ears. He has shaped the passage, however, by changing the length of the lines and linking them by rhyme, a device not used in Rome, but customary for us. Since bacchiacs cannot be reproduced with the same natural humour as anapaests, they have become anapaests, too; and trochaics and iambics have been made uniform as iambics, a good English rhythm. Although Casson has accepted some simplification of Plautus' spectacular versatility, the translation of the metre comes off well and works effectively with the repetitions and sound patterns that Plautus also included in his effects.

Plautus announces his abundance with the two adverbs of line 574. He continues in line 575 with the two synonymous clauses, each in the same metrical pattern of double anapaest: *neque quod dubitem / neque quod timeam;* and he ends the line with alliteration. The essentially prosaic organization of this lyric reveals itself in lines 576–9 in the three successive clauses linked by explanatory *nam*. In line 578, the first four anapaests do produce a rhyming effect, which the final word of line 579 picks up. At the same time, Pseudolus proceeds to develop his military imagery. The first half of line 580 expands on *copias*: the first two words have the same anapaestic pattern; the next two nouns are floridly redundant. Having gotten us to the point of armed conflict at the end of line 580, Pseudolus flamboyantly introduces a parenthetical remark to produce comic suspense, as he boasts of the Roman *virtus* of his non-Roman and probably unknown ancestors and of the crazy 'heroism' embodied in *malitia* and the other rogue virtues he lists; and he slyly moves into bacchiacs to emphasize his impudent boasts. Then, he ends the suspense and resumes the anapaests with two synonymous and metrically identical clauses: *facile ut vincam / facile ut spoliem*. Casson has captured the alliteration and the comic surprise of the line-end with the clause 'phony the foemen.' Now, at line 584 Plautus changes the rhythm to trochees as Pseudolus' crazy confidence grows and his verbiage increases; Casson switches to rhyming iambs that come to their climax in the triple rhyme on Ballio, his method to capture the military pun that Plautus develops from the name. What Plautus has achieved in these lines deserves no Horatian strictures but the greatest admiration, and Casson's translation gives us some means to recapture the admiration that Pseudolus' lively verbal and histrionic performance undoubtedly won from the Roman audience of the 190s.

Now I move to *Bacchides* and the translation of Barsby. The situation is as follows: Mnesilochus, who in angry suspicion at his girlfriend and Pistoclerus has turned the stolen money back over to his father, has now realized his error, that there are two Bacchis-courtesans, and Pistoclerus has fallen for the sister of his beloved. Overwhelmed with disgust at his own credibility and the rashness of his anger, he emerges to voice his despair in heartfelt and patently overdone lyric.

> *petulans, protervo, iracundo | animo, indomito, incogitato,* [tr.] 612
> *sine modo et modestia sum, sine bono iure atque honore,*
> *incredibilis inposque animi, | inamabilis, inlepidus vivo,*

malevolente ingenio natus. postremo id mist quod volo [tr.]
  615
ego esse aliis. credibile hoc est? [anap.]
nequior nemost neque indignior quoi
di bene faciant neque quem quisquam [anap.]
    homo aut amet aut adeat. [iamb.] (lines 612–9)

Barsby has contrived to reduplicate the metre in detail:[15]

Insolent, impudent, angry-tempered, uncontrollable, unreflecting,
Lacking restraint and self-restriction, lacking a sense of right and
    honour,
Disbelieving and demented, disagreeable and unattractive,
Evil-minded: that's my nature, one which, briefly, I prefer
        To see others with. Can you believe it?
There is no one more useless or who less deserves
To get favours from gods or affection from men
        Or even affability.

Mnesilochus does not play the part of a heroic rogue, like
Pseudolus, but of a ridiculous lover whose sufferings provoke
the poet's humour and he our laughter. The techniques of abundance are similar: the first three and a half lines of trochaic
octonarii were probably covered by a single Menandrian trimeter
– two at most. But the abundance of Plautus serves to destroy
the sympathetic role of the despairing lover. Alliteration, and
repetition of initial syllables and of words and metrical struc-
tures, turn this speech into a kind of sing-song. After this trochaic
start, Plautus proceeds to short anapaestic lines of very prosaic
content – much more simply and aptly done, no doubt, by
Menander – which are ostentatiously prosaic in Barsby's version.
The two comparatives give some shape to line 617, and the
succession of *nequior ... neque ... neque* organizes lines 617–8. The
pair of verbs in assonance and iambic rhythm, with which Plautus
closes his lyrical period, yields in Barsby to the pair of nouns in
assonance: 'affection ... or ... affability.' Thus, Plautus uses his
metrical and comic genius to create one lyric of abundance where
the rogue-slave struts and boasts and wins our approving laugh-

ter for his intrepidity; and in *Bacchides* he uses analogous techniques to let a young man emote and elicit a laughter that registers our alienation: we do not joyously share the rogue's energy here; we laugh at the verbose self-pity of a man who depends upon another's roguery.

Menander, according to Plutarch's anecdote, developed his general conception for his comedies, and thereafter he considered the play composed: the actual words that would embody that conception would follow. Plautus, it seems clear, operated in quite a different manner and developed a kind of comedy where the words and metre take priority over inherited plot and give shape to a comic conception that differs sharply from that of the Greek New Comedy. Instead of naturalistic speech patterns, couched in the simplest of iambic metres, all in the service of a rich series of dramatic themes that represent our basic humanity and our need to control ourselves by reason and self-awareness to live responsible lives as members of a cooperating family – as Menander elegantly worked out his art – Plautus centres his comedy on words: words spoken in voluble abundance, relished by speaker and audience alike for their sound, repetitiveness, metrical forms, and the sheer confidence that they represent in the speaker as to the importance of his or her being, whether boasting, tricking, or emoting in amatory agony. Menander shrinks from the overweening language and behaviour that violates average humanity; Plautus features characters who overact and talk outrageously and aim for a special superhuman status.

The lover moans that he suffers like some mythological victim of divine torments, a Pentheus or a toiling Hercules; the angry father rants at the deceptions he has incurred with an uncontrollable, hysterical rage; and the rogue-slave boasts of his trickery and the (normally) temporary 'triumph' he enjoys as though *malitia* transforms him into a heroic superman. Words, metre, and the appropriately exaggerated comic actions establish this Plautine kind of comedy. The plot of the Greek original exercises little control over Plautus in his maturity, and the dramatic themes which were essential to the original conception must succumb to Plautus' comic emphasis on anarchic pleasure and roguish triumph. And finally Plautus takes the subdued and realistic representation, which was enacted on stage without express awareness of the audience, as though it 'mirrored' life itself, and turns it into a highly self-conscious performance that continuously involves the Roman audience. As Plautus out-talks reality and his Greek originals, as he flaunts his numberless numbers and lets his characters rollick in musical comedy, and as he compels everyone to overact and to seek to triumph over normal existence and achieve superhuman status (if only for a moment), he wins over his audience, no doubt all too willing from the start to revel in this special Roman manipulation of words. And now it is time to turn away from this verbal mastery to the audience which Plautus addressed and won. What was Plautus' 'contract' with it? What did the audience get from these comedies and their verbal and metrical abundance?

CHAPTER SIX

Plautus and His Audience: The Roman Connection

In the finale of the comedy *Pseudolus*, the enterprising slave, who has accomplished a series of successful deceptions against a soldier's aide, a pimp, and finally his old master Simo, returns from celebrating his success with his friends. He is quite happily drunk. Staggering towards centre stage, he starts to address his recalcitrant feet: 'Hey, what is this? Now then, feet, what's going on here? Are you going to stand or not? Or do you want someone to come and pick me up off the ground? Damn it, if I fall down, there'll be trouble for you. Are you going to keep going forward? Aha, I'm going to have to get angry with you today ... That's the trouble with wine: it trips up the feet first: it's a tricky wrestler ... Wow, I really am pickled!' (lines 1246–52).[1]

Reeling and swaying, Pseudolus describes the celebration he has enjoyed in slurred but intelligible speech. He had delivered to his amorous young master, Calidorus, the prostitute he had swindled from the pimp: there were girls (i.e., whores: *scortis*, line 1271) for the other males, including the slave, and they all began joyously to live it up, with drink, sex, and dancing. What a wonderful thing it was to be unanimous in the spirit of pleasure, to be free of all grim faces and stupid moralization! However, he has returned to the door of his master Simo, because Simo owes him a large sum of money, 20 minae, on a bet that Pseudolus would never get the girl Phoenicium away from the pimp.

Simo is the usual angry, miserly old man of Plautine comedy, and it pains him terribly that he must pay off this irritatingly smart slave of his, but he has one major consolation: the pimp has confidently bet him the same sum in the same terms, and has already reluctantly forked over the money. Simo, therefore, has steeled himself to pay Pseudolus and, by having the money ready, he hopes to deprive Pseudolus of some of the exultation and the chortling that he knows will be dumped on him. (He hopes also, perhaps, to prevail on the slave to give him some of the money back.) When Pseudolus staggers up to the door and starts pounding on it and loudly calling for Simo, the master quickly emerges, for he easily recognizes, he says, the 'voice of the worst of men.'[2]

He does not, however, expect to find Pseudolus in quite so outrageous a condition. 'What's this I see?' he asks; and the slave replies impudently: 'Your man Pseudolus, drunk and crowned with a garland,' (line 1287). After Simo, in an aside to us, expresses his shock and his perplexity as to how to handle this unruly slave, Pseudolus continues, still more impudently, with a sly parody of a conventional greeting: 'I a bad man am visiting a perfect man' (vir malus viro optimo obviam it, line 1292). Simo decides to make the best of the situation and politely replies, 'May the gods bless you, Pseudolus,' but his self-control explodes when the staggering slave loudly burps in his face.[3]

We are plainly watching and hearing a situation in which the master and slave relation is being reversed. Normally, it is the master who unashamedly gets drunk and expects the slave to tolerate his grossness, but here Pseudolus acts the part of shamelessness.[4] Presuming on this role, the slave now demands his money from Simo and expects Simo not only to load the bag of gold on his shoulders, but also to follow him subserviently through the streets of Athens. When Simo objects, Pseudolus utters the famous motto of all victors: 'Tough luck for the conquered' (vae victis, line 1317).[5] Simo accepts his humiliating defeat and the reparations he must pay, and at the end Pseudolus half-promises to return some of his prize. With this final hope, Simo then goes along with his slave to join the drunken and amorous celebrations we have already heard described (lines 1328–31). He has been totally co-opted into the licentious world of pleasure that has been Pseudolus' goal throughout the play, a goal in direct opposition to everything that Simo, as an avaricious and angry old man, has pursued.

Now, the question I am asking in this chapter is: What is the Roman connection? What does this adaptation of Greek comedy, worked as it is in Plautus' particularly ingenious fashion, mean for Plautus and his Roman audience in the first decade of the second century BC? In previous chapters, I have been edging us towards that question. The first chapter described the confrontation between Plautus and Menander as one between equals; I argued, using especially *The Bacchis-Sisters* as my example, that Plautus possessed the artistic talent and comic vision to criticize his most distinguished Greek predecessor, Menander, and to 'deconstruct' his plays, that is, to reject specific elements of Menandrian comedy and to change it constructively into something with an entirely different, but thoroughly valid, ethos. Thus, Plautus takes a play where the Greek family under paternal authority was all important, where irresponsible pursuit of selfish and impermanent and expensive affairs with prostitutes would be checked and a wayward, amorous son be obliged to return to the family and accept marriage with a girl approved by father and Athenian society; and the Roman creates a comedy where the paternal authority is discredited and, first, a slave, then, a pair of courtesans take over and assert the dominant authority in life of pleasure and self-indulgence. Accordingly, instead of the father bringing his shamed son home from the courtesan, she seduces the father as well as the son into her house. Similarly, in subsequent chapters, I have argued that Plautus shaped Philemon's and Diphilos' comedies to his purposes and replaced the dominant romantic theme of his Greek predecessors by upstaging lovers.

When we left behind the Greek connection, our attention focused on one of the most important comic achievements of Plautine theatre: the creation of what I called the 'bad' hero and the development of a rich, increasingly significant theme of heroic badness over the course of a career of a quarter-century. I represented this Plautine hero/heroine in the familiar category of a rogue, self-consciously proud of his/her badness and eagerly confronting and conquering the loudly trumpeted but increasingly discredited qualities of the authority figures of the comic world. Since all audiences can respond to and side with well-designed and -acted roguery, it was possible for the moment to treat this

rogue-hero and his or her plot of deception and victory over
conventional figures of power and wealth as a timeless theme,
just as we can read as a timeless general myth the medieval
stories about Reynard the Fox or the stories Joel Chandler Harris
put together in the American South and attributed to a black
narrator called Uncle Remus, stories about Bre'r Rabbit, who
was even smarter than Bre'r Fox.[6]

The fact is, though, that timeless themes do have local and
temporal connections, and Plautus' response to Menander was
not just that of a great comic poet satisfying his own private
sense of artistic propriety. Plautus was composing his comedies
in a specific time and place and for a specific audience, and so
the Roman connection is as important as, if not more important
than, the Greek connection; and Plautus' awareness of his Roman audience, the special relation he created with the *spectatores*
over the years, becomes the necessary subject of this last chapter. To state our problem concretely, we want to determine, if
possible, what these deconstructed Greek comedies and these
rogue-heroes meant to Plautus as a comic dramatist in his time
and place and what they were supposed to mean – and apparently
succeeded in meaning, to judge from Plautus' long successful
career – to his contemporary Roman audience.

Anyone who reads a Plautine comedy or, better still, sees a
performance of a play of his realizes that Plautus was a dramatist who regularly worked to produce a direct relation between
himself and the audience.[7] Since such intrusion by the comic
poet and similar interruptions by comic characters to appeal to
the audience have become stock features of modern TV comedy,
it perhaps needs to be emphasized that Plautus' practice was
unusual. Neither Menander, his Greek predecessor, nor Terence,
his Latin successor (who reverted to many discarded Greek practices, from conscious and well-considered preference), intrudes
on his plays himself or allows his characters to step out of the
dramatic context, break the illusion, and chat with the audience.
The many ways in which Plautus furthers his intimacy with the
assembled Romans have been well studied. He starts in the prologue, where there is one, or alternatively in the opening scene.
Even though the playwright does not speak the prologue, he

plainly projects onto the speaker issues and concerns which involve the audience less with the speaker (often a marginally involved deity) than with the poet and his ideas about his comedy.

Whereas Menander's prologues concentrate on getting the play going, by quickly setting the scene and giving necessary background details, without byplay between speaker and audience or ironic comments about dramatic practices, Plautus in the fifteen prologues (for twenty plays) regularly talks to his Roman audience about listening intently, sitting quietly, and being attentive; flatters them as Romans; jokes with them about their business dealings, and the like; he uses the occasion to give the name of the play and its original Greek title and poet; he sets the scene, ostentatiously transporting his spectators to Athens or the occasional alternative locales; and, where the background is somewhat complex, he provides relevant information, what he calls the *argumentum*, and necessary data as to how twins are to be distinguished or impersonators are to be recognized. That is a lot of business to be done, and usually the playwright carries it off with a certain nonchalance and confidential smile that lets us in on an important secret: he does not take this Greek play very seriously. Why should he give the name of the Greek original and its poet, except to imply that the whole thing is non-Roman but that he is doing his best to adapt this alien material? Why does he expose the illusion of setting the scene, if it is not to emphasize the geographical and ideological distance between Rome and Athens?

In the prologue of the *Menaechmus Twins*, we hear these lines: 'This is what comic poets regularly do: they claim that all the events take place in Athens, so that the play will seem more Greek to you. I'll tell you it's happening nowhere but where it is. So this plot is Greek, but not Attic: it's Sicilian,' (lines 7–12). The speaker then embarks on his *argumentum* (lines 17 ff), which starts with the kidnapping of a Syracusan twin baby – he parenthetically interrupts his narrative (lines 22–3) to insist that he never had any direct experience of the details, but relies on an informant, again distancing himself and us from the situation. After telling us what happened in Syracuse as the result of the loss of the one twin and how the other grew up, he announces that he must betake himself on foot to Epidamnus in order to continue 'authentically' (lines 49–50). (The lost twin had ended up there, but the reference to the 'Sicilian plot' has suggested that the scene of action would be Sicily.) Playing with this scenic illusion, he asks if anyone in the audience has business which he'd like done for him while the speaker is in Epidamnus – of course, for a fee; but anyone who paid would be a credulous fool (lines 51–5). He returns to his background details after this sabotaging interruption, and then concludes with more ironic business about the setting: 'This city is Epidamnus,' he declares (and we should imagine that he clearly indicates with a gesture the actual city of Rome in which the Greek play is being performed), then goes on: 'as long as this play is being staged. When another play is staged, it will become another town,' (lines 72–3).

This deconstructed illusion about the setting in a Greek land serves not only to establish Plautus' distance from his chosen dramatic situation, but to ensure that the Roman audience shares this alienation, that both feel a sense of superiority in their alienation. The audience are not supposed to lose their self-awareness as Romans, sitting in a temporary and uncomfortable theatre in Rome and watching very strange doings, very un-Roman behaviour. Even in his late play, the *Truculentus*, Plautus started off his prologue exploiting the joke about the setting. 'Plautus petitions a paltry portion of land within your great and gracious gates, where he may assemble without architects Athens' (lines 1–3). My translation cannot capture all the alliteration and word play, so I shall cite the Latin: *perparvam partem postulat Plautus loci / de vostris magnis atque amoenis moenibus, / Athenas quo sine architectis conferat.* Here, the speaker does not pretend to transport the audience away from everyday Rome to Greece, but rather to bring Athens to Rome.

Among some recent admirers of Plautus, much has been made of what are called metatheatrical techniques and themes.[8] It is very useful to emphasize the ways in which Plautus calls attention to the stage fiction, breaks and exposes the dramatic illusion, favours plots of deception where illusion is openly manipulated, and creates characters who themselves enjoy the power of flamboyant dramatic poets staging their own shows and addressing the Roman audience in their turn. However, it is probably prudent to employ this term 'metatheatre' somewhat cautiously in connection with Plautus, so that we don't pretend that he is a poet of the twentieth century, working with metatheatre like Pirandello, Ionesco, or Brecht. He is not provoking or exploring large existential questions about the nature of reality and the relativism of illusion; there is absolutely nothing unsettling or unsure for the audience's sense of reality in his comedies. If we must flaunt this voguish term 'metatheatre,' we must confine its usage; and I would particularly emphasize, then, that Plautus' purpose is to distinguish the highly artificial theatre of Athenian comedy, which he has appropriated and altered, from the earthy, roguish comedy of swindles, sex, and sousing which he is staging. As he exposes the theatrical texture of Greek comedy, he moves to another level of theatre, true, but not one that disturbs his Roman audience and leaves it doubtful about reality. On the contrary, the new theatrical level achieved by Plautus confirms the audience in their basic Roman preconceptions: it's better to be Roman than Greek, to live in contemporary Rome than in the incredible, effete Athens of which Menander and his contemporaries wrote. Whether that is a 'higher' or 'better' level of theatre than that of Menander, there is room for disagreement; that it is a different level and the clue to Plautus' success with the Roman audience is what I wish to argue.

I shall be attempting to show that Plautus creates a close rapport with his Roman audience, which in turn is duplicated within the play by the plot and the appealing actions and words of his rogue-stars, so that the spectators achieve what we might call a sense of solidarity as Romans, laughing with the scheming rogues at the victims of their acting skills, a set of fools who are aliens, caricatures developed from Greek theatre and, accordingly, I suggest, representative of Greek weaknesses Romans wanted to believe in. In other words, Plautus' comedies have meaning for himself and his audience because they play with a major issue of his age and of centuries to come, the ideological clash between Greece and Rome, the hate–love, inferiority–superiority ambivalence that characterizes this long and complicated relation.[9] And Plautus basically confirms the Romans in their superiority, for his plots implicitly enact the conquest and defeat of decadent Greece by earthy, roguish, street-wise characters who cherish no idle illusions, inhabit no dream world, but know only too well how to exploit, with wit and highly contagious humour, the egotistic and corrupt illusions of others.

Having established my own plot and, with luck, aligned you with my illusion, let me back off briefly and admit that other theories do exist about the subliminal meaning of Plautine comedy. I shall mention the most common, with the obvious rhetorical purpose of persuading you that they are less likely than my theory. First, the oldest theory can be traced back two thousand years to Horace, but probably could be followed back beyond him to Terence and, no doubt, even to some contemporaries of Plautus. Some sixty years ago, Gilbert Norwood eloquently and incisively revived it.[10] It fixes invidiously on box-office success and sneers that Plautus would do anything to please the customers. Now, I am sorry that Terence had only one popular success and that he had trouble even holding his audience for the duration of a play sometimes. Personally, I love to read and teach Terence; but I won't denounce Plautus' popularity for that reason. Already with Terence, we can see a notable shift away from definitive Plautine stylistic and dramatic features. By the time of Horace, Romans were biased in favour of the polished colloquial style and spare structural economy of Terence, and they had little or no appreciation of Plautus' metrical virtuosity and 'comic opera' lyric songs.[11] However, the bias of early envy and later Augustan stylistic purity should not be allowed to fix on Plautus the snobbish claim that he was knowingly vulgar and appealed only to vulgar tastes with crude comic routines, inconsequential plots, and low language. Plautus was popular because he appealed across the board to Romans of all classes and levels of culture. If we must talk about vulgarity, we must recognize that Plautine vulgarity functions as a necessary element of his fundamental plot or myth, the ideological clash between the corrupt and arrogant representatives of family authority and prosperity and, in contrast, the earthy (vulgar, if you insist) roguish heroes with whom, by Plautus' comic art, we are solidly aligned. Thus, rejecting the snobbery of the critics, I would dismiss the stigma of 'vulgar popularity' and rephrase it as sensitivity to the Roman ethos, ability to dramatize a key concern of Roman self-consciousness. (We really don't know that Plautus made much money from the theatre, only that he was repeatedly staged, even after his death.)

The other theories are more modern. Dunkin and others, for example, have suggested that Plautus dramatizes a social conflict between slaves and slave-exploiters, that the comedies represent a protest against Greek and Roman slave societies.[12] That explains (to their thinking) why Plautus creates slave-heroes: he takes a polemic position (as an ex-slave himself perhaps) against Roman slave-owners. Although superficially attractive, this theory has convinced few. Rome had not become a thorough slave society at the end of the third century, and anything like collective guilt over slavery or an Emancipation Movement was entirely out of the question.[13] Moreover, Plautus' slave-heroes are, as we saw in chapter 4, but a phase in his development of rogue-heroes who are not slaves, namely, free though socially inferior prostitutes, parasites, and even wives. Finally, if such were indeed the purpose of Plautus, to espouse the cause of slaves, it is difficult to imagine how the aediles would have paid to stage such controversial comedies year after year and not easy to conceive of what part of the audience this theme would please. It seems to me that Plautus could feature slaves as heroes who defeat their masters precisely because the audience was not threatened by such a plot, because, then, not protecting a prevailing slave interest it could even identify with the rogue-slave and regard the stupid master as an alien, non-Roman.

Although slavery was probably not a major issue in Rome at this time and so not unsuitable for comic material, it has been argued that some of the many political problems of this exceedingly turbulent period could have been and were noticed by Plautus.[14] There was the war with Carthage and Hannibal, which dominated the final decades of the third century; and new wars followed in Greece and Asia Minor during the early second century. There was the rivalry among various ambitious families, each seeking to advance its own interests by dextrous use of clients, factions, and even the poets. There were changes in morality and lifestyle after the Carthaginian War ended, a sudden and predictable relaxation of tension, growth of consumer goods, and importation of luxury items. A reaction set in among the conservative thinkers against extravagance and moral laxity, and Cato advanced his fortunes and weakened the Scipiones on such issues. There were some exotic religious movements, and one of these, the Bacchanalian worship, seemed so anti-Roman and pernicious that it was hounded out of Italy in 186 BC. Such exciting times surely could have stimulated the partisan wit of a political poet. It appears that an older comic poet, Naevius, had attempted to launch an attack on the powerful aristocratic family of the Metelli some time around 206. For his unwise efforts, Naevius ended up in the stocks, a sign of the power of the Metelli and a warning to other partisan poets.[15] Plautus probably alludes to this poet's punishment in passing (Miles, lines 210–12), but he certainly does not side with Naevius. And that is almost the only likely contemporary political allusion in the comedies that scholars can agree on. Thus, although optimistic conjectures have been made that certain plots veil comments on Scipio or Cato or the rights of women, the consensus of readers remains that Plautus worked a non-political vein of basic comedy with his audience.

A more interesting theory about the basis of Plautus' agreement with his audience is that of Erich Segal in his clever book *Roman Laughter*. Segal adapts a general theory of comedy as psychological release to the occasion on which Roman (like Greek and Medieval European) comedies were performed, namely, holidays.[16] Relying on the comic studies of Cornford (on Aristophanes) and Barber (on Shakespearean comedy),[17] he suggests that the Roman festivals were privileged occasions of freedom and pleasure, in sharp contrast to the prevailing grim and 'Puritanic' atmosphere of daily Rome. Thus, the greedy, ill-tempered fathers in Plautus' plays should be felt as caricatures of the *paterfamilias*, the all-powerful figure of authority in the Roman family; and the Plautine rebels, the amorous sons and the rogue slaves and prostitutes. represent the restless victims of this oppressive paternalistic scheme. When in the typical Plautine plot the greedy father is deceived or exposed as a would-be adulterer, worse than his son, and when the normally subordinate social elements – sons, slaves, and whores – prove to be smarter and more adept in dealing with comic reality, that, according to Segal, represents a holiday dream, a momentary indulgence of freedom before everyone returns to the everyday authoritarianism of cheerless Rome.

The problem with Segal's theory is not with his analysis of Plautus, but with his portrait of Roman society in Plautus' time and then his assumption of how the comedy fits Roman society. For example, he makes Cato the Censor the symbol of the entire era. Apart from the fact that Cato became censor in the final year of Plautus' life and an important figure in Roman politics only at the start of the second century, a decade at least after Plautus' dramatic career had become successful, it is not valid to think of Rome as a Puritanic society over the entire quarter-century of Plautus' activity. The war years produced one kind of social climate, perhaps restricted but not restless: the war tended to unite Romans of all ages, and the sons of fighting age were, of course, very precious in the eyes of their families, not the silly, shiftless types that people Plautus' comedies in that period and every period. The postwar years allowed various reactions against the straitened circumstances of wartime: there were some years of great freedom, then some years of moderation or conservative crack-down. That Rome itself, even under Cato, was ever grim and utterly cheerless strikes me as most improbable. After all, Cato himself was famous for his clever wit. Finally, the careers of young men and older fathers were so different, in Rome, from those of the characters in this inherited Greek comedy, that it was not likely that the audience would identify these Greek domestic problems as Roman allusions. It should be remembered that Plautus' comedies produce caricatures of both sons and fathers, no more sympathetic to the silly sons than to their silly fathers, except that the sons pursue pleasure. But the major change by Plautus, the creation of a new 'hero' to replace father and son, really has no function in Segal's theory about Rome (though he ably analyses its purely comic functions).[18] Accordingly, while Segal did make some important observations on the mechanics of Plautine comedy, his view of Roman society in Plautus' day seems to me historically flawed, and that vitiates his account of how the comedy worked with the Roman audience.

And that brings us back, by default (I hope), to the theory that I wish to advance. The problem with the rejected theories is that they presuppose some kind of divided sentiments in the Roman audience, and therefore that Plautus would be pleasing one group or faction and displeasing another, depending on what partisan issue or what area of Roman dissatisfaction he had espoused. My suggestion is that the comedies enact an ideological conflict that pits, not one Roman interest against another Roman interest, but rather Roman sense of self-identity in the audience as a whole against their biased feelings, whetted by Plautus, about Greek civilization. One test of my theory is the issue of war and soldiers. Plautine soldiers tend to be fools, unsuccessful and victimizable rivals-in-love of the young amorous master.[19] Their folly consists typically of empty boasting about their heroic exploits and incredible assurance that all women find them desirable. Plautine slaves, in contrast, when they play the 'hero,' regularly adopt military metaphors and strut about as though they are consuls at war in command of Roman legions and in quest of bloodless victory and much plunder. Now, how do we sort out this dialectic between foolish real soldiers and roguish metaphorical 'conquerors'?

Some years ago, I wrote a paper on The Braggart Soldier, the only Plautine play where the soldier has a major role and gives the title.[20] There are good reasons to date it about 205, which means that it is one of the earliest surviving comedies. It also means that it was composed during the later stages of the Second Carthaginian War, just after Roman forces had inflicted a disastrous defeat at the Metaurus River on Hannibal's brother, who was trying to join Hannibal with crucial reinforcements. That victory turned the tide of the war. The next year (204), young Cornelius Scipio would be sent off with an army to invade North Africa and force Hannibal to withdraw from Italy, then in 202 to encounter Scipio in set battle in defence of Carthage at Zama. Roman victory at Zama ended the military threat of Carthage. Knowing this historical context and suspecting even that the comedy might have been performed for the special victory celebrations after the Battle of the Metaurus, I did not then dare suggest that the foolish soldier symbolized Plautus' and Roman public opinion's feelings about Roman militarism. But I did want him to represent some negative Roman experience, so I suggested that he embodied the unhappiness and resentment that arises in the civilian population during a long war: unhappiness over the loss of family members, over farms that had been overrun and burned by Hannibal's troops in Italy; bitterness at the number of sacrifices demanded of the non-combatants; resentment of some of the soldiers who, like this braggart, came home on leave, told tall tales of danger and heroic feats, and stole the girls away. Well, that's not so bad an idea, and I dare say that many Roman civilians entertained divided feelings about the war. However, I am now sure that Plautus was not mainly trying to tap those divided feelings. The principal function of the soldier is to represent a ridiculous and non-Roman kind of soldier and soldiering, at which the entire audience, as Romans, can join in laughing. Plautus appeals to Roman solidarity.

The soldier is a Greek mercenary, fighting for money, not for any principle, certainly not in defence of his home and country against a national enemy. That sets him drastically at odds with Roman soldiers, who were conscripted in times of emergency.[21] There were Greek mercenaries in Hannibal's armies, and Roman soldiers had encountered such mercenaries in numerous battles during the third century, losing some engagements but always winning the war in the end. The plot of the comedy takes this male braggart and symbolically unmans him: it exposes him as a liar and coward, as an unromantic and unattractive fool who is brought to the verge of castration, condign punishment for his silly male egotism and his gullible leap into entrapment as an adulterer. The mercenary soldier emerges as the very opposite of the Roman soldier: he represents, in fact, the contemptible features of Greek corruption. Now it becomes obvious why Plautus attributes to the clever slave, who engineers the humiliation of the soldier, metaphorical terms connected with Roman military practice. Palaestrio, by his intrepid wit, exhibits basic qualities with which the Roman audience identifies, and when the military imagery is added by the poet, Palaestrio becomes a victorious exponent of the Roman ideological conflict with tired but still boastful and glaringly corrupt Greek civilization.

Now let us go back to Pseudolus and his moment of triumph, where we left him some time ago. The first part of his success involves the deception of a soldier's military aide by the rapacious name of Harpax. After displaying his totally superior intelligence over the soldier, despite the comic disparity between the flamboyant military dress of Harpax and the very unsoldierly look and attire of the slave, Pseudolus appropriates the war imagery of the 'heroic' slave. 'I shall now lead out my legions,' he declares, 'under these standards, all in ranks, with favorable omen and good augury according to plan, and I have total confidence that I shall be able to destroy my enemies,' (lines 761–3).[22]

The second military victim of Pseudolus' campaign proves to be the pimp Ballio. We have already heard the slave boasting of his plans to besiege and storm the fortress represented by the pimp (even though at the time he hasn't the foggiest notion of a scheme) and, as if to build his own confidence, he has punned on the name and declared that he will make a fine ballistic assault on Ballio: *Ballionem exballistabo lepide* (line 585). In fact, once the soldier plays into his hands, Pseudolus can then easily take the next step against the pimp, using a friend in disguise to bilk Ballio of the prize, his prostitute. Here is the moment to ask the thematic question again: what does it mean to Plautus and his Roman audience when they see a clever slave 'heroically' swindle a pimp? In what sense, as even Simo suggests, is Pseudolus an 'epic' Ulysses who has stolen the precious Palladium from the citadel of Ballio (sc. Troy, line 1064)?

Segal is, of course, correct when he emphasizes the antipathetic qualities of the pimp, an enemy of pleasure, a profiteer from love, and regularly a swindler of young lovers.[23] However, whereas he seems to imagine that the pimp is somehow allied with the cheerless everyday qualities of Rome in Plautus' day, I think it more correct to view Ballio and his fellow pimps as a hostile, alien element. The linguists are not in entire agreement about the words *leno* and *lena* (respectively, 'pimp' and 'bawd' in Latin), but they seem convinced that they are not native Latin words, were borrowed from a neighbouring culture, and first make their appearance in extant texts as of Plautus' earliest plays.[24] I am sure that the second-oldest profession was well in place in Archaic Rome long before the second century, but not in the organized manner of Ballio's flagrantly Greek establishment. In my view, it is significant that Plautus takes a very benevolent attitude towards individual prostitutes (far more so than humane and generous Menander), but makes pimps the target of comic attack, the victims of the rogue's heroism.

From early in the fourth century – and no doubt considerably beforehand – Athenian and Corinthian prostitutes and the industry that centred on their attractions prospered sensationally, and the luxury trade of prostitution became a major topic of Middle Comedy, to judge from pages and pages of excerpts in Athenaeus.[25] The topic, sentimentalized and humanized, continued into New Comedy. But Rome, even at the end of the third century, had in no way reached the stage of luxury and pleasure that had existed in Greece for two hundred years. It would get there, yes, but we must not confuse the pages of Petronius and the whore-houses of Pompeii with the state of Roman civilization in Plautus' time. Just as the mercenary soldier of Greece strikes the Roman mind as a degenerate, so the pimp and his organized business, I believe, would appear to the Roman audience another proof of Greek perversion, commercialization and base profiteering from the management of prostitutes. The rogue who outwitted a slimy pimp, whether he were a slave like Pseudolus here, and Toxilus in the *Persa*, or a free-born parasite like Curculio, so long as he mainly helped another, the helpless young lover, and merely enjoyed the success of cleverness, would earn the approval of the audience and, in a comic way, enact the imagined superiority of undeveloped Rome over hypertrophic Greece.

However, the major representative of Greek inferiority in Plautine comedy is the deconstructed angry or libidinous father, the character who in the original Greek plays serves as the focus of legitimate moral authority. Menander and his fellow Greek poets supported a rationale of society which emphasized the central importance of the family and of the father as the final arbiter of family needs and values. Menander's fathers tend to be forbearing, gentle, concerned for family feelings, and honourable in their practical efforts to advance the family fortunes.[26] They are not avaricious or pointedly materialistic; they get deceived, but without our laughing approval of the deception; and when they do get angry, it is over a major ethical issue affecting the entire family, not over being tricked and made a laughing-stock. Although the Roman family was also the heart of Roman values, and the Roman *paterfamilias*, if anything, even more of a revered authority figure than the Greek father of the fourth century, Plautus refuses to adapt the honourable Greek figure to an equally respectable position in his Latin versions. Plautine fathers become the very essence of the corrupt qualities against which the heroic and energetic heroes conduct their successful 'battles.'

Simo, the master of the household who becomes Pseudolus' final victim, has his personality defined at his first appearance (lines 415 ff). He comes on in conversation with another older man who, because of his general leniency and good humour, emphasizes by contrast the harsh and angry nature of Simo. Simo has no good qualities: Plautus has reduced him to a stereotype of selfish, irritable negativity, preoccupied with money rather than people. His entrance speech reveals much. Irately, he declares that, if the wastrels and lovers chose a dictator to represent their interests in Athens, his son Calidorus would win election hands down. Rumours are circulating about the boy and his efforts to borrow money to buy free his prostitute-friend, and Simo seethes with fury, convinced of the truth of the rumours, not at all concerned to talk to his son and work things out carefully. As the older friend points out, Calidorus is acting like any normal young Greek, indeed precisely as Simo did when he was that age (line 437). But the father is not ashamed to be a hypocrite: his avaricious conservativeness now needs no defence or apology, in his mind.

As in the case of *The Bacchis-Sisters*, Plautus does not stage an encounter between father and son, having no intention to dramatize sympathetically the generational tensions. Instead, he now introduces Pseudolus as the representative of the son's interests, the comic 'hero' who takes on the 'villain.' Simo quickly transfers his anger from his son to Pseudolus, and this anger is all the stronger because he correctly regards the slave as the brains behind the silly son's efforts to find money. We witness a striking clash of personalities: angry Simo, who cannot control his fury, versus smooth, smiling Pseudolus, who consciously acts a part and skilfully manipulates Simo, because of his anger, into the actions he wants.[27] Simo is prepared to expect a tissue of lies from his tricky slave. What Pseudolus does to baffle him is to tell the truth – like the Delphic Oracle, he impudently claims (line 480). As if to taunt Simo with his Greek limitations, Pseudolus even answers the master's questions in simple Greek. Once Simo has confirmed the fact that his son is trying to figure out with Pseudolus how to bilk him of the necessary price for the girl, he sneeringly asks the slave: 'Well, what are you going to do now, since I'll never give you the money, forewarned as I am?' (lines 504–5). Pseudolus then smoothly foretells what he is in no position to guarantee at this time, but ironically what the comic plot allows him triumphantly to fulfil. It constitutes both a challenge and a warning to the master, who leaps into the trap. Here is where he makes a solemn 'contract' with Pseudolus, witnessed by his friend, that, if Pseudolus manages to get the girl away from the pimp somehow, he, Simo, will pay his slave the sum of money which will cover Ballio's loss (lines 535 ff).

The issue, then, is not a moral one, inasmuch as Simo shows no ethical values: he never mentions the family, never expresses moral objections to Calidorus' behaviour, or desire, for example, for the son's marriage and for the future welfare of the household. His only express problems are money and absolute authority. To protect his twenty minae of silver, he eagerly allies himself with the pimp against his son and Pseudolus; and for us that guarantees his culpability and the comic justice of his defeat. By perverting this father into a travesty of grasping materialism, Plautus displaces the positive pole of the comedy. At the same time, he alters the plot and its significance. The Greek father comes to represent negative aspects of contemporary Greek society as encountered by the Romans in their conquest of Southern Italy and then, at the start of the second century, of Greece itself. To the somewhat ignorant and arrogant Romans, it could seem that the Greeks, amidst all their affluence and so-called culture, were so decadent as to be primarily focused on protecting their wealth. Although they couldn't fight and wouldn't work,

Greeks seemed to make extraordinary and base efforts to keep their silver minae. Plautus, then, has turned Simo into a caricature of this negative Greek stereotype which ordinary Romans of this era tended to cherish.

Plautus' deconstruction displaces the moral centre of his comedy from the Greek father (Simo in this play, Nicobulus in *The Bacchis-Sisters*) to the rogue, and he changes the theme from the support of family values to the valid pursuit of personal pleasure outside the family. From the perspective of Simo and the original Greek play, the pursuit of such pleasure is anarchic and hostile. Thus, Pseudolus is the 'worst of slaves' for Simo. But from Pseudolus' perspective – and Plautus makes that our perspective – Simo's 'bad' is our 'good,' and this slave's hostility becomes a heroic Roman campaign against an inferior enemy. In the finale, Pseudolus has earned the right to storm the house of Simo and to treat him with the comic ruthlessness we enjoy: he drunkenly accosts his master, burps in his face, and acts with happy impudence and impunity. And with the lure of money, he gets Simo to leave his home and to follow him to the scene of his son's carousing.

In the end, we may say, I think, that Plautus deconstructs the Greek plays to make them fit his own and his Roman audience's sense of positive humour. Greek domestic values and ethical materialism seem unreal and laughable to Plautus, so he makes them so. He will not let us enjoy the sentimental optimism of Menander or of any other Greek poet. So Plautus transforms the Greek text to adapt it to his occasion, Roman public shows or *ludi* (the Ludi Megalenses of April in the late 190s for *Pseudolus*), and his new hero, the rogue-slave, enacts both the ideological clash and the comic creativity of the poet: he himself stages a comic play for our and his own amusement.[28] As Simo and friend realize, Pseudolus' promised actions against Ballio and his master constitute a dramatic program, and so Simo mockingly sneers: 'Announce the play when you want' (line 546; cf. 552). But soon Simo is amazed to find himself helplessly caught up in Pseudolus' plot, a plot of comic deception over which Simo has lost all control – in which, indeed, he and the pimp end up in the roles of the comic victims, those who are the passive source of our fun. To be made a fool of, a figure of fun (*ludificatus*), is the final reduction of the father Simo, who loves money, like the miser Euclio, more than anything or anyone else. To have managed the fooling is to be the heart of the comedy: the writer of the script, the chief actor, and the impressario who directs others in the plot of one's making. Plautus coins the word *ludificator* for another tricky slave, Tranio of *The Haunted House* (line 1066). Between them, Plautus and his rogues, Pseudolus, the Bacchis-sisters, and the witty wife Cleustrata, inventive and delightful *ludificatores*, have happily had their 'barbarian play,' producing Roman comedy that is, indeed, Roman.

Notes

The following abbreviations of journal titles appear in the notes and bibliography:

AJP	*American Journal of Philology*
CP	*Classical Philology*
CQ	*Classical Quarterly*
CR	*Classical Review*
CW	*Classical World*
ICS	*Illinois Classical Studies*
MD	*Materiali e discussioni per l'analisi dei testi classici*
PCPh	*Proceedings of the Cambridge Philological Society*
QUCC	*Quaderni Urbinati di Cultural Classica*
REL	*Revue des études latines*
RM	*Rheinisches Museum für Philologie*
RSC	*Rivista di Studi Classici*
TAPA	*Transactions of the American Philological Association*
WS	*Wiener Studien*

CHAPTER ONE

1 George Duckworth, *The Nature of Roman Comedy. A Study in Popular Entertainment* (Princeton, NJ: Princeton University Press, 1952)
2 Much of this work was the product of American scholars: R.C. Flickinger, P.W. Harsh, J.N. Hough, H.W. Prescott, and A.L. Wheeler. However, the contributions of W. Beare and W.B. Sedgwick of Great Britain were also highly significant.
3 The inspiration for these studies came primarily from Germany,

from U. von Wilamowitz-Moellendorff, and Friedrich Leo and his admirable students, E. Fraenkel and G. Jachmann. In Toronto, Gilbert Norwood made solid contributions. Also in this proud company, I would readily include P.J. Enk, C.R. Post, and T.B.L. Webster.

4 The Cairo manuscript preserved about three-quarters of *Epitrepontes* (*Arbitrants*), half of *Perikeiromene* (*She Who Was Shorn*) and *Samia* (*Samian Woman*, now virtually completed by the Bodmer papyrus), and the initial fifty lines (plus the valuable hypothesis) of *Heros* (*Hero*).

5 Duckworth, *Nature of Roman Comedy*, 27–38

6 The essential Greek remains of Menander are now conveniently available in *Menandri Reliquiae Selectae*, edited by F.H. Sandbach (Oxford: Oxford University Press, 1972). The volume also includes over four hundred lines of *Sikyonios* (discovered in mummy wrapping in 1964) and substantial additions to *Misoumenos* (*Hated Man*) derived from Oxyrhynchus papyri by Eric Turner up to 1970. Subsequently, in 1977–8, Turner was able to publish more new fragments from the same play. Sandbach has also produced a monumental commentary on the fragments of Menander (Oxford: Oxford University Press, 1973). W.G. Arnott has promised a three-volume edition and translation of the major fragments of Menander; at this point, only volume 1 (London and Cambridge: Loeb Classical Library, 1979) has appeared – a most valuable contribution. For the identification of the Menandrian Greek source of *Bacchides*, see E.W. Handley, 'Menander and Plautus,' University of London Inaugural Lecture, 1968.

7 I shall be using the attractive translation of J. Barsby, which appears in his recent edition of *Plautus. Bacchides* (Warminster: Aris & Phillips; Oak Park, IL: Bolchazy-Carducci, 1986).

8 The enormous bibliography on Menander's and Plautus' comedies begins with Handley's revolutionary lecture of 1968, 'Menander and Plautus.' For relevant bibliography up to 1986, see Barsby's edition of *Bacchides*. See also the special chapter in N.W. Slater, *Plautus in Performance: The Theatre of the Mind* (Princeton, NJ: Princeton University Press,1985), 94–117.

9 In the fourth act of *Dyskolos*, when Knemon is brought in after being saved from the well, a changed man, the metre changes to trochaics for his speech (lines 708–47) and the remaining thirty-five lines of the act. In *Samia*, the entire fourth act, which operates at a high emotional pitch from beginning to end and contains the

dénouement, uses trochaics (lines 421–615).

10 Plutarch, *Moralia*, 712c, indicates that Menander regularly plotted a young man's affair with a hetaira so that he either abandoned it by the end of the play or he (and she) were allowed to continue their genuine, if impractical, relationship for a while. See my article, 'Love Plots in Menander and His Roman Adapters,' *Ramus* 13 (1984), 124–34.

11 On Plautine sons' death-wish for their parents, especially their fathers, see E. Segal, *Roman Laughter* (Cambridge, MA: Harvard University Press, 1968), 17 ff.

12 Handley, in 'Menander and Plautus,' was the first to point out these puns in connection with Plautus' change of the slave name Syros in Menander. Note especially line 240: *opus est chryso Chrysalo* ('Chrysalus needs gold'); and lines 361–2: *credo hercle adveniens nomen mutabit mihi/facietque extemplo Crucisalum me ex Chrysalo* ('I believe that, when he comes, he'll change my name and make me, instead of Chrysalus, Crucisalus, e.g., The Mounter of the Cross'). On Plautus' special use of crucifixion humour, see Holt Parker, 'Crucially Funny or Tranio on the Couch: The *Servus callidus* and Jokes about Torture,' *TAPA* 119 (1989), 233–46.

13 Lines 1087–95 in Barsby's translation

CHAPTER TWO

1 Cf. W.G. Arnott, 'A Note on the Parallels between Menander's *Dyskolos* and Plautus' *Aulularia*,' *Phoenix* 18 (1964), 232–7. Arnott assumed it as a fact that Menander wrote the original of the Plautine play, and he cited a substantial number of articles that agreed with him. More recently, however, he concluded that the resemblance between the two plays was attributable to the fact that Menander was influenced by Alexis' *Lebes*, which Arnott then believed to be the original of Plautus' play. See his 'The Greek Original of Plautus' *Aulularia*,' *WS* 101 (1988), 181–91, and 'Alexis' *Lebes*, Menander's *Dyskolos*, Plautus' *Aulularia*,' *QUCC* 33 (1989), 27–38. R.L. Hunter, 'The *Aulularia* of Plautus and Its Greek Original,' *PCPh* 207 (1981), 37–49, voiced much hesitance on this question.

2 See *Asinaria*, lines 10–12, and *Miles*, line 86 (in its delayed prologue).

3 See Mark L. Damen, 'The Comedy of Diphilos Sinopeus in Plautus, Terence, and Athenaeus,' Dissertation, University of Texas, 1985, and James Astorga, 'The Art of Diphilos: A Study of Verbal Humor

in New Comedy,' (Dissertation, University of California, Berkeley, 1990.

4 *Florida*, line 16

5 Found in its basic form, the story of these two friends appears in Iamblichus, *De vita Pythagorica*, lines 23A ff (supposedly as it was told to Aristoxenos by Dionysios himself).

6 Aristotle *Ethica Eudemia*, 7.2.14 ff, and *Ethica Nichomachea*, 8.3 ff

7 *De amicitia*, 51

8 *Mercator*, lines 588 ff

9 Cf. line 933, with its reference to Cyprus and the father's decision to send Charinus into exile: none of these details corresponds with actual facts of the play, but each serves as a flamboyant allusion to tragic myth.

10 *Trinummus*, lines 374 ff. I have discussed this passage and others from this comedy in my article, 'Plautus' *Trinummus*: The Absurdity of Officious Morality,' *Traditio* 35 (1979), 333–45. See also the analysis of the same lines by N. Zagagi, *Tradition and Originality in Plautus: Studies of the Amatory Motifs in Plautine Comedy*, Hypomnemata 62 (Göttingen: Vandenhoeck und Ruprecht 1980), 90–104.

11 Cf. lines 688–91.

12 Cf. lines 698 ff.

13 Cf. lines 763 ff.

14 I have discussed one portion of Gripus' lyric solo, in which he and Plautus misinterpret, I think, a contemporary allusion in Diphilos because of the military associations of the name. See 'Gripus and Stratonicus: Plautus' *Rudens* 930–936,' *AJP* 107 (1986), 560–3.

15 Plautus, presumably following Diphilos, has Trachalio grab the rope as soon as he notices what Gripus is carrying, in order to get him to stop and give an account of the origin of the trunk. From the moment that Trachalio enters, then, Diphilos dramatizes, by action as well as words, the antagonism of the two slaves. D. Konstan, *Roman Comedy* (Ithaca, NY: Cornell University Press, 1983), 73 ff, has studied the slaves' conflict for the way it exhibits the problem of cultural boundaries.

16 It is assumed that Diphilos, in conformity with the 'three-speaker convention,' plotted movements this way, removing Trachalio so that Palaestra could assume the more sentimental role for the recognition. Plautus, in contrast, crowds his stage with five speakers, including both Trachalio and Palaestra. But Trachalio functions only as the spiteful antagonist of Gripus during the recognition.

17 Cf. lines 1184 ff.

18 Cf. S. Charitonidis, L. Kahil, and R. Ginouves, *Les Mosaïques de la maison de Ménandre à Mytilène, Antike Kunst* Beiheft 6 (1970). In a triclinium and portico of a house dating to the third century AD are some fifteen illustrations of Menandrian comedy, one per play. The one numbered 7 identifies itself as a representation of Act II of *Epitrepontes.*

19 Chalinus wishes that Olympio's lot would suffer the same fate as befell the lot of the descendants of Heracles, when they disputed the possession of Messenia with Cresphontes. In that myth, Cresphontes' biased brother, who was overseeing the lot drawing, used two different clay lots for the contestants. That of the Heraclids, consisting of sun-dried clay, dissolved once it was immersed in the water. Hence, the lot of Cresphontes, being of baked clay and unaffected by the water, had to be drawn, giving the victory to Cresphontes, thanks to the corrupt brother.

20 For the special way that Plautus handles Chalinus, without resorting to the stereotypes that modern critics mistakenly attribute to the character, see my 'Chalinus *armiger* in Plautus' *Casina,' ICS* 8 (1983), 11–21.

21 At her first entrance, Cleustrata confidently voices her suspicions of Lysidamus as lusting after Casina: cf. lines 151 ff, and especially line 195 (*sed ipsus eam amat*).

CHAPTER THREE

1 S.G. Ashmore, *The Comedies of Terence, edited with introduction and notes* (Oxford: Oxford University Press, 1910), 5.

2 See Leo Salingar, *Shakespeare and the Traditions of Comedy* (Cambridge: Cambridge University Press, 1974), and Karen Newman, *Shakespeare's Rhetoric of Comic Character. Dramatic Convention in Classical and Renaissance Comedy* (New York: Methuen,1985).

3 Ovid, *Tristia,* 2.369: Plutarch, *Amatorius (Moralia* 763b), cited by Stobaeus, 4.20.34, who, however, says more than our present text of Plutarch. He seems to attribute to his source this statement: 'One thing there is that gives birth to all the plays of Menander alike: love, which acts like a breath of life in common to them.' He then goes on to argue against the irrationality of love, citing the same passage of Menander that Plutarch does, but giving eight lines where Plutarch provides only two.

4 Plutarch, *Moralia* 777f, which I have discussed in 'Love Plots in Menander and His Roman Adapters,' *Ramus* 13 (1984), 124–34

5 See chapter 1, 26. For Plautus' treatment of love in general, see P. Grimal, *L'Amour à Rome* (Paris: Hachette, 1963) [= *Love in Ancient Rome*, tr. A. Train, Jr (New York: Crown 1967; University of Oklahoma Press, 1986)], especially chapters 3 and 4, on love and marriage and courtesans.

6 See chapter 2, 40.

7 The similar lyrical soliloquy by the young lover at the opening of the anonymous *Mostellaria* is one of several reasons that lead some scholars to assign it to Philemon.

8 See chapter 2, 46.

9 Marriages do result from the developments in *Trinummus* and *Casina*; however, neither their Greek writers, Philemon and Diphilos, nor Plautus, their adapter, makes matrimony the essential goal of either plot.

10 Cf. Terence, *Adelphoe*, line 486. At line 473 in *Andria*, Glycerium (who has not been raped, but is pregnant) delivers her one line, which is so formulaic that suspicious old Simo assumes that she is faking a birth.

11 At the start of the *Dyskolos*, Menander, who has used a god in the prologue, as is done in *Aulularia*, then introduces the young lover Sostratos and favourably characterizes his love.

12 Molière borrowed and developed this comic scene in Act V of *L'Avare*. Bergson, in his admirable essay, '*Laughter*,' described this device as one of 'reciprocal interference.'

13 It is Molière who expands the mutual incomprehension by letting each character use, in different ways, the word 'treasure,' the miser quite literally, the lover metaphorically.

14 One of these summaries states that Euclio (apparently having at last realized the negligible value of riches) gave the money (a kind of dowry?) as well as his daughter to Lyconides. I consider that ending (at least, as it is simplistically understood) unlikely. Molière may come closer to the intention of Plautus with his version, where Harpagon the miser, true to his 'idée fixe,' ignores all his family as he happily clutches his recovered wealth. Konstan (*Roman Comedy* [Ithaca, NY: Cornell University Press, 1983]), in his chapter on the *Aulularia* (pp. 33 ff), studies the miser's alienation from his community and the city-state.

15 For useful studies of this comedy, see W. Süss, 'Zur Cistellaria des Plautus,' *RM* 84 (1935), 161–87; W. Ludwig, 'Die plautinische

Cistellaria und das Verhältnis von Gott und Handlung bei
Menander,' *Ménandre: sept exposés* (Geneva: Fondation Hardt,
1970), 43–110; G. Thamm, '*Zur Cistellaria des Plautus*,'
(Dissertation, University of Freiburg, 1971); and Konstan, *Roman
Comedy*, 96 ff.

16 Palinurus drops from the play after line 321; Curculio has just
appeared, forty lines earlier, at 280, and rapidly taken over the chief
role of comic energy.

17 I refer to the young man here. The old lover always had to give up
his foolish love and return to his marriage.

18 For the basic anthropological formulation of Plautine plots, see
M. Bettini, 'Verso un' antropologia dell' intreccio,' *MD* 7 (1982), 39–
101. Slater's analysis of Toxilus as lover and rogue (*Plautus in
Performance: The Theatre of the Mind* [Princeton, NJ: Princeton
University Press, 1985], 55 ff) is useful.

19 On Pseudolus' diverse qualities as a rogue, see chapters 4 and 6.

20 On the incipient rogues of the *Asinaria*, see chapter 4.

21 On Phronesium as a 'flawed rogue' in a satiric comedy, see
chapter 4 and 6.

CHAPTER FOUR

1 I particularly think of P.S. Dunkin, *Post-Aristophanic Comedy:
Studies in the Social Outlook of Middle and New Comedy at
Both Athens and Rome* (Urbana: University of Illinois Press, 1946)
[= *Illinois Studies in Language and Literature*, Vol. 31, nos. 3–4].

2 This is the soldier's description of the slave Palaestrio in *Miles*
(line 1374). Pseudolus, in his final triumph, is called *pessimus* by
his master Simo at lines 1285 and 1310, and he has the effrontery
to call himself *vir malus* as he sardonically hails his master with
the phrase *viro optimo* (line 1293). Pseudolus, in his turn, hails his
ally Simia as a man who could not be worse (*peiorem*) or 'more
deviously bad' (lines 1017–18). In the opinion of the pimp Dordalus,
who has been victimized by him, Toxilus the slave is *pessumus
corruptor* (Persa, lines 779). Lyconides rails angrily at his slave in
Aulularia (line 825) as *scelerum cumulatissume*. The rogue, for
Plautus, is superlative in badness.

3 E. Segal has carefully followed out this theme in *Roman Laughter*
(Cambridge, MA: Harvard University Press,1968), Ch. IV, 'From
Slavery to Freedom,' 99 ff.

4 Military *imperium* and a campaign against 'enemies' constitute a

key symbol in the intrigues of *Bacchides* (especially lines 925 ff),
Miles, Persa (especially lines 753 ff), and *Pseudolus*. On the mili-
tant theme in Plautine comedy in general, see J.A.S. Hanson, 'The
Glorious Military,' in *Roman Drama*, (ed. by T.A. Dorey and
D.R. Dudley), 51–85. London: Routledge and Kegan Paul, 1965.

5 Cf. *Bacchides*, lines 1058, 1069, and 1075; *Persa*, line 757; and
Pseudolus, line 588.

6 Pseudolus links *virtus* with his *malitia* at line 581; the slave
Libanus boasts of the success achieved by himself and his fellow-
slave and represents it as a total victory earned by their heroism
(*virtute, Asinaria*, line 556). In later plays, when Plautus casts this
'victory speech' as a lyric hymn, the format itself, no doubt parallel
to that of Roman victory announcements and inscriptions, implies
the presence of *virtus* even in the absence of the word.

7 Menander's slaves regularly possess more experience and practical
wisdom than their masters, and we have a fair number of sententious fragments in which it seems likely that slaves are lecturing
their young masters. However, their actions appear to have been
circumscribed. It is unfortunate that we lack the Greek passages
that followed out the trickery of Syros, the inspiration for
Chrysalus in *Bacchides*. But, as I argue below, the role of Daos in
Aspis shows how a trickster in Menander is a loyal slave working
for the family, not what Plautus would have made him: a rogue
challenging the family structure and supporting anarchy and
dissipation.

8 What I call the Aristophanic rogue has been ably analysed by
C.H. Whitman in *Aristophanes and the Comic Hero* (Cambridge,
MA: Harvard University Press, 1964).

9 Lines 128 ff. Note how Shakespeare abandons heroic verse as soon
as the king leaves the stage; Falstaff speaks in unheroic prose.

10 The saying about 'he who fights and runs away' is not Shakespearean. In the thirteenth Centennial edition of *Bartlett's Quota-
tions* (Boston and Toronto: Little, Brown, 1955), 69a, the first
definite form of the expression is credited to Tertullian; but
Menander may have used it four hundred years earlier. At the end
of Scene 3, just before leaving, Falstaff declares: 'Give me life;
which if I can save, so; if not, honour comes unlooked for, and
there's an end.'

11 Scene 4: 'The better part of valour is discretion; in the which better
part, I have saved my life.'

12 It is significant that Shakespeare excludes Falstaff from the final

scene (5), which he casts in heroic verse and uses to bring the battle
to a dignified conclusion.

13 My translation

14 Similarly, Pseudolus is the heroic force in the play named after
him, and so the 'victory celebrations' of the finale centre on him.

15 Soon after the *Aspis* was first published, I wrote an article in which
I suggested that Daos, in lines 399–420, performs in his role as
trickster like the *servus currens* of Plautus. See *Phoenix* 24 (1970),
229–36. Although I still believe that the excited and overacted
running of Daos, as he mouths tragic lines from Euripides and other
dramatists, anticipates the histrionic running entrance of the
Plautine slave, I must agree with others now who argue that
Menander himself was thinking back to the stereotype of the 'tragic
messenger.'

16 In the tattered remains of Act IV, at lines 506 ff, the editors assume
that the soldier knocks at the house-door, which Daos opens and
thus becomes the first to greet his returned master.

17 *Asinaria*, lines 267 ff. Leonida moves briefly into military metaphors at lines 269–71. For recent studies of this play, see D.
Konstan, *Roman Comedy* (Ithaca, NY: Cornell University Press,
1983), 47 ff, and N. Slater, *Plautus in Performance: The Theatre of
the Mind* (Princeton, NJ: Princeton University Press, 1985), 55 ff.

18 *Miles*, lines 219 ff

19 See John Wright, 'The Transformations of Pseudolus,' *TAPA* 105
(1975), 403–16, and Slater's chapter (*Plautus in Performance*, pp. 118
ff) that develops and modifies the invaluable groundwork of Wright.

20 In the light of Sander Goldberg's recent article on this play,
'Plautus' *Epidicus* and the Case of the Missing Original,' *TAPA* 108
(1978), 81–92, in which he argues the possibility that Plautus may
have composed it without any specific Greek source (apart from the
general conventions of New Comedy), the unique ending, freedom
for the rogue-slave, makes sense as Plautus' invention. Slater
(*Plautus in Performance*, 19 ff), in his chapter on this play, argues
that it celebrates in the slave Epidicus 'the powers of self-creation.'

21 Nicobulus continues to demand vengeance against Chrysalus up to
line 1187, after which he collapses under the seduction of Bacchis.
In his analysis of the comedy, Slater (*Plautus in Performance*)
emphasizes Chrysalus, and he explains the slave's departure as one
of significant choice that defines the total superiority of his role. As
he reads lines 1072–3 (pp. 112–13), Chrysalus declares his refusal to
continue in his role. I prefer to think that Plautus himself is

preparing us for the abandonment of the clever slave and his final stress on the courtesans.

22 Cf. the epithets (*pessumae, mala*) applied to the courtesans in *Bacchides*, lines 1122 and 1162, and the comic alliterative terms of line 1167, *probriperlecebrae et persuastrices*.

23 Konstan (*Roman Comedy*), in his chapter on this play (pp. 142 ff), rightly calls it 'satiric comedy,' See also Cynthia Dessen, 'Plautus' Satiric Comedy: The *Truculentus*,' *Philol. Quarterly* 56 (1977), 146–58. See also P. Grimal, 'A propos du Truculentus. L'anti-féminisme de Plaute,' *Mélanges Marcel Durry* (Paris: Belles Lettres 1970), 85–98.

24 On Chalinus, the slave who poses as Casina and thus promotes the disgrace of the husband, yet, in my opinion, plays a subordinate role, unlike the typical Plautine rogue, see my article, 'Chalinus *armiger* in Plautus' *Casina*,' *ICS* 8 (1983), 11–21. Slater (*Plautus in Performance*), in his chapter on this play, ably traces the way Cleustrata seizes control of the plot in the second half (pp. 84 ff).

CHAPTER FIVE

1 Plutarch, *Moralia*, 347e. It must be conceded that the prologues of Terence's six comedies do supply us with considerable information about the controversies in which he became involved as he struggled to gain and maintain recognition for his kind of drama. However, his statements there are polemical; they lack the interest of a pointed anecdote, and, in any case, suggest that Terence, like his model Menander, put the premium on elaborate composition. Hence, his arguments over *contaminatio*. On Terence as the exception to the development of Roman comedy and Plautus as its very heart, see John Wright, *Dancing in Chains: The Stylistic Unity of the Comoedia Palliata* (Rome: American Academy in Rome 1974). On Terence's prologues, see Sander Goldberg, *Understanding Terence* (Princeton, NJ: Princeton University Press, 1986), ch. 2 (31 ff).

2 In *Poetics*, 6, Aristotle says that plot is the first principle, so to speak the 'soul', of tragedy. Characterization and diction are secondary features. Aristotle may have modified this doctrine somewhat in connection with comedy, but his views on comedy remain in dispute for lack of sure evidence. If he argued from Aristophanes and Old Comedy, he would not necessarily have stressed plot as much as he did for tragedy; if he argued from the

new trends in Middle Comedy, the prevailing comic form of his
mature years, he could very well have insisted on the priority of
plot. For the most recent discussion of this problem and the
relevance of the Coislinian Tractate, see Richard Janko, *Aristotle on
Comedy: Towards a Reconstruction of Poetics II* (Berkeley: University of California Press, 1984), 214 ff.

3 The prologue of Moschion in Menander's *Samia* provides the
clearest comparison. Somewhat damaged, it still limited itself to
eighty-five to ninety lines, lines that were superbly crafted to let
Moschion present himself as an interesting and sympathetic
character as he was sketching out his complex and affectionate
relationship with his foster father, Demea. He addresses the
audience, but he does not play up to them.

4 For some of the ways in which Plautus modified and sabotaged the
sympathetic aspects of the young lover of Philemon's *Emporos* as
he developed his overacting, overemoting Charinus, see chapter 2,
40 ff.

5 It is a topos of consolatory literature that, when a young man has
died prematurely – in combat, by accident, or in sickness – the gods
have acted to rescue him from all the troubles of a long life. I
believe that Menander therefore adapted a Greek commonplace, in
the mouth of a sententious slave, to his comedy (and that Plautus
twisted it into an outrageously laughable context). In an interesting
reuse of Menander's passage, Plutarch cites the line as part of his
Consolation to Apollonius, 119e.

6 For the restricted role of the *servus currens* in Terence, see the
modest routine assigned to Geta, running in with news which makes
him irate and anxious, in *Adelphi,* lines 299 ff, and the severe
strictures on a rival's extravagant treatment of the part in *Heauton-
timorumenos,* lines 31–2. For the strictly controlled representation of
anger in the abused and deceived father, see the depiction of Chremes
in *Heauton,* lines 915 ff; though he claims to be out of control with
fury at line 920, he quickly moves on to rational response. Cf. also
the calculated reaction of angry Demea in Act V of *Adelphi.*

7 Aulus Gellius 1.24.3

8 Horace, *Ars poetica,* 270–2

9 See F. Perusino, *Il tetrametro giambico catalettico nella commedia
greca* (Rome: Ed. dell' Ateneo, 1968), 129 ff. We know that
Menander did not confine the metre to the dénouement and its
developments in Acts IV and V. He also used it in Act II of *Perikeir.*
and Act III of *Sikyonios.*

10 Duckworth's chapter 'Meter and Song,' in his *Nature of Roman Comedy* (Princeton, NJ: Princeton University Press, 1952), 361–83, provides valuable data and discussion.
11 Cf. *Miles*, lines 1011–93.
12 *Mercator*, lines 335–63. This long soliloquy introduces the scene where Charinus encounters his father for the only time in the comedy, and each deceives the other without realizing that he deals with a rival. During Charinus' speech, Demipho enters and silently observes him, but cannot – as the convention would have it – make out the words that we can easily hear. Thus, his puzzled comment at the end of the speech, at line 364.
13 The only other instances of initial lyric occur in the mature plays, *Epidicus* and *Persa*. The latter also works up to a flamboyantly lyric finale of drunken triumph among the slaves.
14 Lionel Casson, *Six Plays of Plautus* (New York: Anchor Books, 1960), 285. This excellent translation has gone out of print.
15 John Barsby, *Plautus, Bacchides* (Warminster: Aris & Phillips; Oak Park, IL: Bolchazy-Carducci 1986), 61 ff.

CHAPTER SIX

1 *Quid hoc? sicine hoc fit, pedes? statin an non? | an id voltis ut me hinc iacentem aliquis tollat? | nam hercle si cecidero, vostrum erit flagitium. | pergitin pergere? ah! saeviendum mi hodie est; | magnum hoc vitium vino est: | pedes captat primum, luctator dolosust. | profecto edepol ego nunc probe habeo madulsam.* The translation is adapted from E.F. Watling, *Plautus: The Pot of Gold and Other Plays* (Harmondsworth: Penguin 1965), 264.
2 *vox viri pessumi me exciet foras* (line 1285)
3 In response to Simo's greeting at line 1294, the manuscripts assign Pseudolus the monosyllabic *hae!* What that means can only be determined by Simo's angry reaction (which serves as a stage direction to the man playing Pseudolus' role): *quid tu, malum, in os igitur mi ebrius inructas?* (line 1295).
4 Besides this scene, the most obvious example of drunkenness in Plautus may be found in the reeling entrance of Callidamates, supported by his slave-girl friend Delphium, in *Mostellaria*, lines 313 ff. It is a commonplace of New Comedy that too much wine, combining with erotic desire (*vinum et amor*), constitutes an excuse for an act of rape, so long as the repentant young rapist subsequently marries his victim.

5 The phrasing, of course, is peculiarly Roman. Thus, Livy uses it in 5.48.9 as he describes the capture of Rome by the Gauls in 390 BC; supposedly, the arrogant Gallic chieftain spoke these words to the defeated and helpless Roman leaders! Varro also made the title of one of his satires from this expression.

6 Needless to say, these tales of heroic rogues, animals or slaves or criminals, possessed special applications in their times and social context. Cf. the legend of Robin Hood or the stories of the 'heroic' English privateers at the time of the Spanish Armada. See also M.M. Bakhtin on Rabelais' rogue culture: *Rabelais and His World* (Moscow: Khudozh Litteratura, 1965; Cambridge, MA: MIT Press, 1968).

7 See W.R. Chalmers, 'Plautus and His Audience,' *Roman Drama*, ed. by T.A. Dorey and D.R. Dudley, 21–50 (London: Routledge and Kegan Paul, 1965); also G.E. Duckworth, *The Nature of Roman Comedy* (Princeton, NJ: Princeton University Press, 1952), 132 ff, on 'the violation of the dramatic illusion.'

8 See, especially M. Barchiesi, 'Plauto e il "metateatro" antico,' *Il Verri* 31 (1970), 113–30; G. Petrone, *Teatro antico e inganno: finzioni Plautini* (Palermo: Palumbo 1983); and N. W. Slater, *Plautus in Performance: The Theatre of the Mind* (Princeton, NJ: Princeton University Press, 1985), ch. 9, 'Playwriting as Heroism' (168 ff).

9 That this ambivalence about Greek culture and contemporary Greek decadence was a principal issue of Plautus' day hardly needs to be argued. It is represented in the behaviour and words of two key Roman politicians of the age, Scipio Africanus, the Hellenophil conqueror of Hannibal, and Cato, who posed as a stern, rigid anti-Greek moralist. On Plautus' application of current attitudes towards the Greeks, see the three differing judgments – in *Dioniso* 46 (1975) – of E.W. Handley, 'Plautus and his Public: Some Thoughts on New Comedy in Latin' (117–32); of P. Grimal, 'Jeu et vérité dans les comédies de Plaute' (137–52); and of W.G. Arnott, 'Plauto, uomo di teatro' (203–17).

10 G. Norwood, *Plautus and Terence* (New York Longmans, 1932), p. 19: 'The comment of Horace is definite [citing *Epistulae*, 2.1.176 ff]: "See how slipshod is Plautus as he hurries across the boards – he is eager to drop the cash into his purse, and then he cares nothing whether his play tumbles or stands upright." We are to see later how entirely this is justified – save as to the poet's greed. The construction of some among his plays is so incredibly bad that even

stupidity alone, even indifference alone, seem insufficient to explain it. We can but suppose that he neither knew nor cared what a drama is, and was concerned with nothing save to amuse an audience that knew and cared not indeed less, but no more.' On the same page, Norwood also cites Horace's criticism of Plautus' metres and use of wit, found in *Ars poetica* (270–2).

11 Horace no doubt expected most of his readers to agree with him when, in *Ars poetica* (270–2) he sneered at the ancestral Romans of the early second century who praised Plautus, calling their praise too tolerant, not to say stupid.

12 P.S. Dunkin, *Post-Aristophanic Comedy: Studies in the Social Outlook of Middle and New Comedy at Both Athens and Rome* (Urbana: University of Illinois Press, 1946)

13 Although Rome had acquired slaves during the third century by its conquests in Southern Italy and then its defeat of Carthage in the First Punic War, the big expansion of slavery began in the early second century (i.e., after Plautus' death), when Roman armies, having again defeated the Carthaginians in 202, were then free to expand their conquests in Greece and the Eastern Mediterranean. See W.L. Westermann, *The Slave Systems of Greek and Roman Antiquity* (Philadelphia: American Philosophical Society, 1955), and Keith Hopkins, 'The Growth and Practice of Slavery in Roman Times,' in *Conquerors and Slaves* (Cambridge: Cambridge University Press, 1978), 99–132, P. Spranger, *Historische Untersuchungen zu den Sklavenfiguren des Plautus und Terenz* (Stuttgart: F. Steiner, 1984), voices deep scepticism about the utility of Plautus for historical inferences. See also J. Dingel, 'Herren und Sklaven bei Plautus,' *Gymnasium* 88 (1981), 489–504.

14 The American Philological Association addressed the subject recently (1982) in a panel on 'topicality in Plautus.' See P. Harvey, 'Historical Topicality in Plautus,' *CW* 79 (1986), 297–304. E.S. Gruen has a very sensitive chapter entitled 'Plautus and the Public Stage' in his *Studies in Greek Culture and Roman Policy* (Leiden: E.J. Brill 1990), 124–57. He emphasizes that the Roman attitude towards Greece was not sheerly invidious but ambivalent, and that Plautus' comedy reflects that ambivalence.

15 The circumstances of Naevius' arrest are far from clear. He may have involved himself in partisan politics on the side of Fabius and his defensive strategy, at a time when the more aggressive methods of the Metelli carried the day. The senarius which Pseudo-Asconius and others preserve, 'By fate [i.e., not justice or merit] the Metelli

have become consuls in Rome,' does not sound especially irritating or slanderous, hardly up to the level of vehemence of most Roman invective. Therefore, it seems difficult to believe that such a verse could have landed Naevius in prison. Either he must have said many worse things or he did some illegal things which the consuls could punish.

16 E. Segal, *Roman Laughter* (Cambridge, MA: Harvard University Press, 1968)

17 F.M. Cornford, *The Origin of Attic Comedy* (Cambridge: Cambridge University Press, 1914 [1st ed.], 1934 [2d ed.]); C.L. Barber, *Shakespeare's Festive Comedy* (Princeton, NJ: Princeton University Press, 1959). Segal (*Roman Laughter*) added some material also, from Freud and Freudian followers, on holidays and the superego.

18 Segal (*Roman Laughter*) does focus on the theme of achieving liberty for the slave and the reversal of power for the master, but he interprets these themes primarily in connection with his principal interest, the festive or Saturnalian spirit of temporary freedom in comedy. Thus, his rogue is not a spokesman for Rome against Greece, but for freedom from puritanic, Catonian repression.

19 See J.A. Hanson, 'The Glorious Military,' in *Roman Drama*, ed. by T.A. Dorey and D.R. Dudley, 51–85 (London: Routledge and Kegan Paul, 1965). Menander's soldiers have more character, and, instead of being the target of intrigue, often prove to be the legitimate and sympathetic romantic heroes. Cf. *Misoumenos, Perikeiromene, Sikyonios.* See W. T. Mac Cary, 'Menander's Soldiers: Their Names, Roles, and Masks,' *AJP* 93 (1972), 279–98.

20 The lecture, given to the University Centers in Georgia in 1982, entitled 'Plautus' First Dramatic Success,' was not published at the time, but put aside to mature here. In the meantime, I came to know the article of E.W. Leach, 'The Soldier and Society: Plautus' *Miles Gloriosus* as Popular Drama,' *RSC* 28 (1980), 185–209. Leach also examines the relevance of the ridiculous soldier to Roman society in 205 BC and rejects the notion that Plautus voices an antimilitaristic or antiwar viewpoint. See also the discussion of R. Perna, *L'originalità di Plauto* (Bari: 'Leonardo Da Vinci,' 1955), 195 ff.

21 Greek and Persian armies employed mercenaries as hoplites through much of the fourth century and throughout the third, in the wars of Alexander's successors. It is for one of them, a Seleucid king (line 75) that the braggart has been fighting, obviously as a hoplite, in parts of Asia Minor (Cilicia 42, Cappadocia 52). See

G.T. Griffith, *The Mercenaries of the Hellenistic World* (Cambridge: Cambridge University Press, 1935). By contrast, throughout the Republic, the Roman army depended on citizen-soldiers (as regulated by law) to serve in the legions (the equivalent of Greek hoplites as the fighting strength of the army). See G.R. Watson, *The Roman Soldier* (Ithaca, NY: Cornell University Press, 1969), 39. It is true, however, that the Romans did hire foreign *auxilia* to make up for their deficiency in cavalry and light-armed forces. Numidian cavalry, therefore, played a crucial part at Zama in 202, the final victory of the war being waged at the time Plautus completed the *Miles*. Nevertheless, nobody would mistake a Numidian horseman for the kind of heavily armed foot-soldier that Plautus makes this braggart to be.

22 *omnis ordine his sub signis ducam legiones meas / avi sinistera, auspicio liquido atque ex sententia; / confidentia est inimicos meos me posse perdere.*

23 On the pimp as an 'agelast,' one who is hostile to laughter and fun, see Segal, *Roman Laughter*, 79 ff.

24 Devoto had conjectured that the word came from Etruscan. Although it certainly is true that the Etruscans shocked the early Romans by their seemingly outrageous sexual libertinism and probably helped to stimulate prostitution at the start, the likelihood of an Etruscan origin of the words *leno, lena* does not receive support from either A. Walde and J.B. Hoffmann, *Lateinisches Etymologisches Wörterbuch* (Heidelberg: Carl Winter, 1938) or A. Ernout and A. Meillet, *Dictionnaire étymologique de la langue latine*, 4th ed. (Paris: Editions Klincksieck, 1979). The latter work declares of the word *leno*: 'Sans doute emprunté. Non roman.' And both seem to incline for a Greek source.

25 See my article 'Corinth and Comedy,' in *Corinthiaca: Studies in Honor of D.A. Amyx*, ed. by Mario A. Del Chiaro, 44–9 (Columbia: University of Missouri Press, 1986).

26 See W.T. MacCary, 'Menander's Old Men,' *TAPA* 102 (1971), 303–25. MacCary aptly points out (p. 323) that we know of no lustful old man (father) in Menander's surviving works, and 'one wonders about Plautine changes' in such plays as *Bacchides*. But other Greek poets did feature the *senex amator*, as we know, for instance, from Philemon's original of *Mercator* and Diphilos' original of *Casina*.

27 See the influential article by John Wright, 'The Transformations of Pseudolus,' *TAPA* 105 (1975), 403–16, and N.W. Slater, *Plautus in*

Performance: The Theatre of the Mind (Princeton, NJ: Princeton University Press, 1985), ch. 7.

28 Pseudolus compares himself to a poet in inventiveness as he desperately casts around to find a way of starting his intrigue against Simo and the pimp: *nunc ego poeta fiam* (line 404). Cf. the boast of the women at the end of *Casina*, that no poet has ever produced a more artful deception than they have (lines 860–1).

Bibliography

Anderson, W.S. 'A New Menandrian Prototype for the *Servus currens* of Roman Comedy.' *Phoenix* 24 (1970), 229–36
– 'Plautus' *Trinummus*: The Absurdity of Officious Morality.' *Traditio* 35 (1979), 333–45
– 'Chalinus *armiger* in Plautus' *Casina*.' *ICS* 8 (1983), 11–21
– 'Love Plots in Menander and His Roman Adapters.' *Ramus* 13 (1984), 124–34
– 'Corinth and Comedy.' In *Corinthiaca. Studies in Honor of D.A. Amyx*, ed. by M. Del Chiaro, 44–9. Columbia: University of Missouri Press, 1986
– 'Gripus and Stratonicus: Plautus' *Rudens* 930–936.' *AJP* 107 (1986), 560–3
Arnott, W.G. 'A Note on the Parallels between Menander's *Dyskolos* and Plautus' *Aulularia*.' *Phoenix* 18 (1964), 232–7
– 'Young Lovers and Confidence Tricksters.' *University of Leeds Review* 13 (1970), 1–18
– 'Menander, Plautus, Terence.' *Greece and Rome New Surveys* 9 (1975), 1–62
– 'Plauto, uomo di teatro,' *Dioniso* 46 (1975), 203–17
– *Menander*. London and Cambridge, MA.: Loeb Classical Library, 1979), Vol. 1
– 'The Greek Original of Plautus' *Aulularia*.' *WS* 101 (1988), 181–91
– 'Alexis' *Lebes*, Menander's *Dyskolos*, Plautus' *Aulularia*.' *QUCC* 33 (1989), 27–38
Ashmore, S.G. *The Comedies of Terence*. Oxford: Oxford University Press, 1910
Astorga, James. 'The Art of Diphilos: A Study of Verbal Humor in New Comedy.' Dissertation, University of California, Berkeley, 1990

Bakhtin, M.M. *Rabelais and His World*. Moscow: Khudozh Litteratura, 1965; Cambridge, MA: MIT Press, 1968

Barber, C.L. *Shakespeare's Festive Comedy* (Princeton, NJ: Princeton University Press, 1959)

Barchiesi, M. 'Plauto e il "metateatro" antico,' *Il Verri* 31 (1970), 113–30

Barsby, J. *Plautus, Bacchides*. Warminster: Aris & Phillips; Oak Park, IL: Bolchazy-Carducci, 1986

Beacham, Richard C. *The Roman Theatre and Its Audience*. Cambridge, MA: Harvard University Press, 1992

Beare, W. *The Roman Stage*. London: Barnes and Noble, 1965

Bergson, H. *Le rire* (trans. as *Comedy*). New York: Doubleday Anchor, 1956

Bettini, M. 'Verso un antropologia dell' intreccio: Le strutture semplici della trama nelle commedie di Plauto.' *MD* 7 (1982), 39–101

Bieber, M. *The History of the Greek and Roman Stage*. Princeton, NJ: Princeton University Press, 1939

Blänsdorf, J. *Archäische Gedankengänge in den Komödien des Plautus* Hermes Einzelschr. 20, 1967

Buck, C.H. 'A Chronology of the Plays of Plautus.' Dissertation, Johns Hopkins University, 1940

Casson, L. Six Plays of Plautus. New York: Anchor Books, 1960
– *The Plays of Menander*. New York: New York University Press, 1971

Chalmers, W.R. 'Plautus and His Audience.' In *Roman Drama*, ed. by T.A. Dorey and D.E. Dudley, 21–50. London: Routledge and Kegan Paul, 1965

Charitonidis, S., L. Kahil, and R. Ginouves. *Les mosaïques de la maison de Ménandre à Mytilène (Antike Kunst* Beiheft 6, 1970)

Cody, J.M. 'The *senex amator* in Plautus' *Casina.*' *Hermes* 104 (1976), 453–76

Cornford, F.M. *The Origin of Attic Comedy*. Cambridge: Cambridge University Press, 1934

Damen, M.L. 'The Comedy of Diphilos Sinopeus in Plautus, Terence, and Athenaeus.' Dissertation, University of Texas, 1985

Dessen, C.S. 'Plautus' Satiric Comedy: The *Truculentus.*' *Philol. Quarterly* 56 (1977), 145–68

Dingel, J. 'Herren und Sklaven bei Plautus.' *Gymnasium* 88 (1981), 489–504

Dover, K.J. *Aristophanic Comedy*. Berkeley: University of California Press, 1972

Duckworth, G.E., 'The Dramatic Function of the *servus currens* in Roman Comedy.' In *Classical Studies Presented to E. Capps*, 93–102. Princeton, NJ: Princeton University Press, 1936
– *The Nature of Roman Comedy*. Princeton. NJ: Princeton University Press, 1952
Dunkin, P.S. *Post-Aristophanic Comedy: Studies in the Social Outlook of Middle and New Comedy at both Athens and Rome*. (Urbana: University of Illinois Press, 1946
Enk, P.J. 'Terence as an Adapter of Greek Comedies.' *Mnemosyne* 13 (1947), 81–93
Ernout, A., and A. Meillet. *Dictionnaire étymologique de la langue latine*, 4th ed. Paris: Editions Klincksieck, 1979
Fantham, E. 'The *Curculio* of Plautus: An Illustration of Plautine Methods in Adaptation.' *CQ* 15 (1965), 84–100
– 'Sex, Status, and Survival in Hellenistic Athens: A Study of Women in New Comedy.' *Phoenix* 29 (1975), 44–74
– 'Philemon's *Thesauros* as a Dramatisation of Peripatetic Ethics.' *Hermes* 105 (1977), 406–21
– 'Plautus in Miniature. Compression and Distortion in the *Epidicus*.' *Papers Liverpool Latin Seminar* 3 (1981), 1–28
Flickinger, R.C. *The Greek Theatre and Its Drama*. Chicago: University of Chicago Press, 1926
Forehand, W.E. 'Plautus' *Casina*: An Explication.' *Arethusa* 6 (1973), 233–56
Fraenkel, E. *Plautinisches im Plautus* (Berlin: Weidmann, 1922)
Gaiser, K. 'Die plautinische *Bacchides* und Menanders *Dis Exapaton*.' *Philologus* 114 (1970), 51–87
– 'Zur Eigenart der römischen Komödie: Plautus und Terenz gegenüber ihren griechischen Vorbildern.' *Aufstieg und Niedergang der römischen Welt*, Bd II (1972), 1027–1113
Galinsky, C.K. 'Scipionic Themes in Plautus' *Amphitruo*.' *TAPA* 97 (1966), 203–35
Garton, G. *Personal Aspects of the Roman Theatre*. Toronto: University of Toronto Press, 1972
Goldberg, S. 'Plautus' *Epidicus* and the Case of the Missing Original.' *TAPA* 108 (1978), 81–92
– *The Making of Menander's Comedy*. London: Athlone, 1980
– *Understanding Terence*. Princeton, NJ: Princeton University Press, 1986
Griffith, G.T. *The Mercenaries of the Hellenistic World*. Cambridge: Cambridge University Press, 1935
Grimal, P. *L'Amour à Rome*. Paris: Hachette, 1963 [=*Love in Ancient*

Rome, tr. A. Train, Jr. New York: Crown Publishers, 1967]
- 'Le Miles Gloriosus et la Vieilesse de Philémon.' *REL* 46 (1968), 129–44
- 'A propos du Truculentus: L'antiféminisme de Plaute.' *Mélanges Marcel Durry*, 85–98. Paris: Belles Lettres, 1970
- 'Le théâtre à Rome.' *Actes du IX Congrès. Assoc. G. Budé*, 1 (1973), 249–305
- 'Jeu et vérité dans les comédies de Plaute.' *Dioniso* 46 (1975), 137–52
Gruen, E.S. *Studies in Greek Culture and Roman Policy*. Leiden: E.J. Brill, 1990
Gurewitch, M. *Comedy: The Irrational Vision*. Ithaca, NJ: Cornell University Press, 1975
Handley, E.W. *Menander and Plautus*. University of London Inaugural Lecture, 1968
- 'Plautus and His Public: Some Thoughts on New Comedy in Latin.' *Dioniso* 46 (1975), 117–32
Hanson, J.A.S. 'Plautus as a Source Book for Roman Religion.' *TAPA* 90 (1959), 48–101
- 'The Glorious Military.' In *Roman Drama*, ed. by T.A. Dorey and D.E. Dudley, 51–85. London: Routledge and P. Kegan, 1965
Harsh, P.W. 'Certain Features of Technique Found in Both Greek and Roman Drama.' *AJP* 58 (1937), 282–93
- *A Handbook of Classical Drama*. Stanford, CA: Stanford University Press, 1944
- 'The Intriguing Slave in Greek Comedy.' *TAPA* 86 (1955), 135–42
Harvey, P. 'Historical Topicality in Plautus.' *CW* 79 (1986), 297–304
Henkle, R.B. *Comedy and Culture: England 1820–1900*. Princeton, NJ: Princeton University Press, 1980
Hopkins, K. 'The Growth and Practice of Slavery in Roman Times.' In *Conquerors and Slaves*, 99–132. Cambridge: Cambridge University Press, 1978
Hough, J.N. 'The Use of Greek Words by Plautus.' *AJP* 55 (1934), 346–64
- 'The Development of Plautus' Art.' *CP* 30 (1935), 43–57
- 'The Understanding of Intrigue: A Study in Plautine Chronology.' *AJP* 60 (1939), 422–35
- 'Link-Monologues and Plautine Chronology.' *TAPA* 70 (1939), 231–41
Hunter, R.L. 'Philemon, Plautus and the *Trinummus*.' *Museum Helveticum* 37 (1980), 216–30
- 'The Aulularia of Plautus and Its Greek Original.' *PCPh* 207 (1981), 37–49

- *The New Comedy of Greece and Rome.* Cambridge: Cambridge University Press, 1985
Jachmann, G. *Plautinisches und Attisches.* Berlin: Weidmann, 1931
Janko, R. *Aristotle on Comedy: Towards a Reconstruction of Poetics II.* Berkeley: University of California Press, 1984
Jocelyn, H.D. 'Chrysalus and the Fall of Troy (Plautus, *Bacchides* 925–978).' *Harvard Studies in Classical Philology* 73 (1969), 135–52
Konstan, D. *Roman Comedy.* Ithaca, NY: Cornell University Press,1983
Law, H.H. 'Studies in the Songs of Plautine Comedy.' Dissertation, University of Chicago, 1922
Leach, E.W. 'The Soldier and Society: Plautus' *Miles Gloriosus* as Popular Drama.' *Rivista di Studi Classici* 28 (1980), 185–209
Leggatt, A. *Citizen Comedy in the Age of Shakespeare.* Toronto: University of Toronto Press, 1973
Lejay, P. *Plaute.* Paris: L. Pichard, 1925
Leo, F. *Plautinische Forschungen zur Kritik und Geschichte der Komödie.* Berlin: Weidmann, 1912
Levin, H. *Playboys and Killjoys. An Essay on the Theory and Practice of Comedy.* Oxford: Oxford University Press, 1987
Ludwig, W. 'Die plautinische Cistellaria und das Verhältnis von Gott und Handlung bei Menander.' In *Ménandre: sept exposés*, 43–96. Geneva: Fondation Hardt, 1970
MacCary, W.T. 'Menander's Old Men.' *TAPA* 102 (1971), 303–25
- 'Menander's Soldiers: Their Names, Roles, and Masks.' *AJP* 93 (1972), 279–98
McLeish, K. *The Theatre of Aristophanes.* London: Thames and Hudson, 1980
Marti, H. *Untersuchungen zur dramatischen Technik bei Plautus und Terenz.* Schellenberg: Winterthur, 1959
Miller, N., tr. *Menander. Plays and Fragments.* Harmondsworth: Penguin, 1987
Newman, K. *Shakespeare's Rhetoric of Comic Character: Dramatic Convention in Classical and Renaissance Comedy.* New York: Methuen, 1985
Norwood, G. *Plautus and Terence.* New York: Longmans, 1932
O'Bryhin, S. 'The Originality of Plautus' *Casina.*' *AJP* 110 (1989), 81–103
Parker, Holt. 'Crucially Funny or Tranio on the Couch: The *Servus callidus* and Jokes about Torture,' *TAPA* 119 (1989), 233–46

Perna, R. *L'originalità di Plauto.* Bari: 'Leonardo da Vinci' editrice, 1955

Perusino, F. *Il tetrametro giambico catalettico nella commedia greca.* Rome: Ed. dell' Ateneo, 1968

Petrone, G. *Teatro antico e inganno: finzioni plautini.* Palermo: Palumbo, 1983

Pöschl, V. 'Die neuen Menander-papyri und die Originalität des Plautus.' *Sitzungsberichte der Heidelberger Akademie* 4 (1973), 5–37

Post, L.A. 'The "Vis" of Menander.' *TAPA* 62 (1931), 203–34

– 'Menander and Terence.' *CW* 26 (1932–3), 33–36

– 'Aristotle and Menander.' *TAPA* 69 (1938), 1–42

Prescott, H.W. 'The Interpretation of Roman Comedy.' *CP* 11 (1916), 125–47

– 'The Antecedents of Hellenistic Comedy.' *CP* 12 (1917), 405–25; 13 (1918), 113–37; 14 (1919), 108–35

– 'Inorganic Roles in Roman Comedy.' *CP* 15 (1920), 245–81

– 'Criteria of Originality in Plautus.' *TAPA* 63 (1932), 103–25

– 'Silent Roles in Roman Comedy.' *CP* 31 (1936), 97–119; 32 (1937), 193–209

– 'Link Monologues in Roman Comedy.' *CP* 34 (1939), 1–23; 116–26

– 'Exit Monologues in Roman Comedy.' *CP* 37 (1942), 1–21

Reckford, K.J. *Aristophanes' Old-and-New Comedy.* Chapel Hill: University of North Carolina Press, 1987

Ryder, K.C. 'The *senex amator* in Plautus.' *Greece & Rome* 21 (1984), 181–89

Salingar, L. *Shakespeare and the Traditions of Comedy.* Cambridge: Cambridge University Press, 1974

Sandbach, F.H. *Menandri Reliquiae Selectae.* Oxford: Oxford University Press, 1972

– (with A.W. Gomme). *Menander: A Commentary.* Oxford: Oxford University Press, 1973

– *The Comic Theatre of Greece and Rome.* London: Chatto and Windus, 1977

Sedgwick, W.B. 'The *Cantica* of Plautus.' *CR* 39 (1925), 55–8

– 'The Dating of Plautus' Plays.' *CQ* 24 (1930), 102–5

Segal, E. *Roman Laughter.* Cambridge, MA: Harvard University Press, 1987

Slater, N.W. *Plautus in Performance: The Theatre of the Mind.* Princeton, NJ: Princeton University Press, 1985

Spranger, P. *Historische Untersuchungen zu den Sklavenfiguren des Plautus und Terenz.* Stuttgart: F. Steiner, 1984

Studemund, W. *Plauti Fabularum Reliquiae Ambrosianae Codicis*

Rescripti Ambrosiani Apographus. Berlin: Weidmann, 1889; repr. 1971
Süss, W. 'Zur Cistellaria des Plautus.' RM 84 (1935), 161–87
Taylor, L.R. 'The Opportunities for Dramatic Performances in the Time of Plautus and Terence.' TAPA 68 (1937), 284–304
Thamm, G. 'Zur Cistellaria des Plautus.' Dissertation, University of Freiburg, 1971
Thierfelder, A. 'Plautus und römische Tragödie.' Hermes 74 (1939), 155–66
Turner, E.G. 'Edition of Menander, Misoumenos 101–466.' Bull. Inst. Class. St. suppl. 17 (1965), and Oxyrhyncus Papyri 23 (1968), 15–55
– 'Edition of Misoumenos 1–92.' Oxyrhyncus Papyri 23 (1968), 56–64
– 'The Lost Beginning of Menander Misoumenos.' Proceedings of the British Academy 73 (1977), 315–31
Walcot, P. Greek Drama in its Theatrical and Social Context. Cardiff: University of Wales Press, 1976.
Walde, A., and J.B. Hoffmann, Lateinisches Etymologisches Wörterbuch. Heidelberg: Carl Winter, 1938
Watling, E.F. Plautus: The Pot of Gold and Other Plays. Harmondsworth: Penguin, 1965
Watson, G.R. The Roman Soldier. Ithaca, NY: Cornell University Press, 1969
Webster, T.B.L. Studies in Menander. Manchester: Manchester University Press, 1950
– Studies in Later Greek Comedy. Manchester: Manchester University Press, 1970
– An Introduction to Menander. Manchester: Manchester University Press, 1974
Weld, J. Meaning in Comedy: Studies in Elizabethan Romantic Comedy. Albany: State University of New York Press, 1975
Westermann, W. L. The Slave Systems of Greek and Roman Antiquity. Philadelphia: American Philosophical Society, 1955
Wheeler, A.L. 'The Plot of the Epidicus.' AJP 38 (1917), 237–64
Whitman, C.H. Aristophanes and the Comic Hero. Cambridge, MA: Harvard University Press, 1964
Wilamowitz-Moellendorff, U. von, Menander: Das Schiedsgericht. Berlin: Weidmann, 1925
Wiles, D. The Masks of Menander. Cambridge: Cambridge University Press, 1991
– 'Marriage and Prostitution in Classical New Comedy.' Themes in Drama 11 (1989) 31–48
Wright, J. Dancing in Chains. The Stylistic Unity of the Comoedia Palliata. Rome: American Academy in Rome, 1974
– 'The Transformations of Pseudolus.' TAPA 105 (1975), 403–16

– 'Plautus (254–184 BC).' *Ancient Writers. Greece and Rome*, vol. I, 501–23. New York: Scribners, 1982

Zagagi, N. *Tradition and Originality in Plautus: Studies of the Amatory Motifs in Plautine Comedy.* Hypomnemata 62. Göttingen: Vandenhoeck und Ruprecht, 1980

Zucker, F. *Freundschaftsbewährung in der neuen attischen Komödie. Ein Kapitel hellenistischer Ethik und Humanität.* Sächsische Akademie der Wissenschaft 98.1, 1950

Index